Latinization and the Latino Leader

"**An important and informative 'how to manual' for 21st century leaders seeking to uncap the massive potential that the Latino/Latina workforce offers business today.** Citing the explosive buying power and cultural influence of Latinos in America, this book is the essential business case and handbook for success in attracting, retaining and advancing Latinos into management and beyond."

> Alison Kenney Paul, *Vice Chairman & US Retail Leader, Deloitte*
> *Past President, Network of Executive Women (NEW)*

"**Vital for any organization that struggles in the hiring, training, retention, and advancement of Latino leadership.** Down-to-earth, ready-to-apply, common- sense advice that hits the mark spot on."

> J.C. Gonzalez-Mendez, *President, McDonald's Latin America*

"**A powerful and practical tool for harnessing and nurturing a critical global resource—leadership!** *Latinization and the Latino Leader* **provides profound insights, concrete resources, and cutting-edge practices that are guaranteed to make a difference.**"

> Chip R. Bell, *best-selling author, most recently of* Take Their Breath
> Away: How Imaginative Service Creates Devoted Customers

"**An incredible resource for excelling with talent management in an increasingly diverse business climate.** *Latinization and the Latino Leader* will help transform your team at every level into advocates of your core culture. It's leadership built on making a difference in every way."

> John R. Patterson, *consultant and best-selling author of*
> Customer Loyalty Guaranteed: Create, Lead, and Sustain
> Remarkable Customer Service

"Marlene is **excellent at assessing the strengths and development needs of individuals, and developing a comprehensive approach to both leveraging their strengths and addressing the developmental needs.** "

> Chere Nabor, *Chief Diversity Officer, Grainger Corporation*

"The challenges faced by Latinos in organizations, particularly in the hospitality and service sectors, make this book an eye opener to the Latinization explosion bringing focus and clarity to engagement and development in the workplace. **A new Latino leader is in the making and the recipe for success is contained in** *Latinization and the Latino Leader.*"

Rick Segal, *General Manager and Managing Director*
Park Hyatt, Chicago

"*Latinization and the Latino Leader* provides **an insightful and necessary understanding of the impact Latinos assert by their contributions daily to the success of the economy in the United States. This is a must read by executives and managers.**"

Maria Sanchez, *President, Organization of Latinos, Exelon West*

"This book is a must read for everyone—Latinos and non-Latinos—to gain knowledge of the new dimensions of multicultural leadership competencies."

Ed Sanchez, *President and CEO, Lopez Foods*

"In an increasingly diverse, interconnected and globalized economy, it's this kind of vision that will help secure America's spot as the world's business leader. **This book will help those Latino leaders navigate their leadership journey**."

Ana Maria Soto, *Executive Director of Latino Initiatives*
National-Louis University

"*Latinization and the Latino Leader* offers staggering statistics on Latinos that every strategic-minded employer should know. It gives you sociological, psychological, and cultural insights on today's Latino leaders as well as practical approaches to strengthening your business by developing your Latino talent. **A must have book for employees and employers alike.**"

Martha Arteaga, *Director of Human Resources, AMLI Residential*

"Cristina Benitez is **a rare combination of both an insightful ethnographer and a savvy marketer,** with a passion for uncovering insights and giving clarity to the Latino emergence in the U.S."

Michael J. Puican, *Associate Director of Corporate Training, DePaul University, former CEO of JossClaude Products*

"If you are looking to gain a competitive advantage, *Latinization and the Latino Leader* provides a road map. Cristina Benitez and Marlene González go behind the scenes of workforce diversity to **explore how to fully integrate the inclusionary environment we are all striving for in our organizations. The key messages are as relevant for all associates as they are for Latinos**."

Carmen Callies-Garcia, *Director, Leadership Development*
SUPERVALU

Latinization

AND THE LATINO LEADER

How to Value, Develop, and Advance
Latino Professionals

Cristina Benitez and Marlene González

Paramount Market Publishing, Inc.

Paramount Market Publishing, Inc.
950 Danby Road, Suite 136
Ithaca, NY 14850
www.paramountbooks.com
Telephone: 607-275-8100; 888-787-8100 Facsimile: 607-275-8101

Publisher: James Madden
Editorial Director: Doris Walsh

Cataloging in Publication Data available
ISBN 13: 978-0-9830436-1-4 | ISBN 10: 0-9830436-1-2

Contents

Acknowledgements

THANKS to the Almighty, our parents, our *abuelitos*, and the fantastic rich mosaic of multicultural and multifaceted Latino culture and heritage that made it possible for us to be proud Latinas and write this book.

Thanks to our spouses Carlos González and Richard Carlson for your love, support and words of encouragement, and critical eye when we were faced by doubts.

Thanks to the unconditional support from all our family members.

Thanks to all Latinos and Latinas professionals and the new generation that made it possible for us to take on this endeavor of writing this book. You added thoughts, experiences, trials, tribulation, contribution, ideas, support, feedback and challenges faced by Latinos in many organizations, government and non-profit.

Thanks to Illivia Yudkin our creative graphic designer, Marcela Landres and Ally E. Peltier our personal editors for your partnership and support. Thanks for great work.

Melody Blass Fisher analyzed, interpreted, and wrote the statistical report. A graduate of Brandeis University with a double major in Psychology and English, she is currently working toward a PhD at the University of Massachusetts in Boston.

Thanks to Cristina Lopez, President of the National Hispana Leadership Institute for making it possible for us to meet at one of your conferences and for your absolute trust, support, and commitment in helping us to conduct interviews and surveys.

Thanks to the entire Mujeres de HACE group at National Louis University for opening your hearts and lives to us and thanks again for sharing your life experiences.

Thanks to respected friends, colleagues, and experts for their profound insights and contributions to this book.

Thanks to the wonderful publishing team at Paramount Market Publishing, Inc., Jim Madden and Doris Walsh, who guided us through the process.

Executive Summary

AMERICAN business leaders can steer the new global paradigm to achieve their highest potential, by understanding how to incorporate inclusion strategies and diversity initiatives to increase their revenue. Recognizing the vital role of Latino employees and consumers is a great place to start—and, in fact, it's essential to your business's success.

Instead of yesterday's "melting pot" model, the U.S. is becoming a "mixing pot," where immigrants from many diverse cultures can retain and celebrate their heritage while they participate in the American dream. The trend away from assimilation and toward acculturation means that Latin Americans are now more likely than ever before to feel they can be their most authentic selves in the workplace. The fastest-growing ethnic group in the U.S., Latinos bring their own unique cultural flavor to the party. And twenty-first century America is witnessing a Latinization explosion: mainstream America has thoroughly embraced Latino food, music, languages, and cultural products. But how does Latinization affect your business's bottom line? The 2000 Census revealed that Latinos currently make up 15 percent of the total U.S. population. Moreover, the Latino population is estimated to account for 45 percent of the total population growth in the U.S. between 2003 and 2013; the Latino labor force is expected to exceed 26 million by 2016. Latinos bring a wide array of cultural constructs, competencies, and traditions to corporate America and Main Street employers. Biculturalism, bilingualism, and core values that include collaboration, respect, and loyalty are just a few of the many skills and attributes Latinos bring to the table. But although Latinization has increased the status and visibility of Latino culture in the U.S., Latino employees still face barriers to their upward mobility: navigating corporate politics, a lack of role models, and misconceptions about Latino culture remain hurdles that emerging Latino leaders encounter in today's workplace.

Latinization and the Latino Leader offers concrete recommendations for manageable, proactive methods to establish or enhance your business's framework to value, develop, and advance Latino employees at every level. Through valuable insights gained from the authors' executive coaching program, examination of relevant statistical data, and a nationwide study of Latino business professionals, *Latinization and the Latino Leader* provides corporate and Main Street employers with solid, hands-on tools to create a culture of inclusion, foster diversity, and reach target consumers. Employers will learn how to achieve material results by capitalizing on their Latino talent to increase productivity and expand their consumer base.

The fact is that a growing Latino population means engaging Latinos is crucial to your bottom line. The key for employers and advertisers alike is in emotionally connecting with their Latino employees and consumers, providing products that resonate and work environments that encourage and develop Latino leadership. The statistics are clear: businesses that focus their messaging to address Latino employees and consumers will enjoy a major competitive edge. But just as important, employers who value and encourage the profound contributions Latino employees make to their organizations can expect to reap the benefits of diverse viewpoints, fresh ideas, and the critical discernment the "Latino lens" provides.

Latino culture is not homogenous or reducible to stereotypes; it is multifaceted and rich in its diversity, and it encompasses the cultures of many countries and peoples. This book is a view of Latino and Latina leaders and their cultural traits for the business leaders of America who seek to understand and connect with their employees and consumers. It is up to the current leadership working in government, on Main Street, in corporations, and in other professional organizations across the nation to reflect the changes apparent in the new and exciting climate of globalization that the twenty-first century has ushered in. This means ensuring that your organization accurately represents the people it serves—our global nation, a tapestry of many cultures and colors. Organizations that embrace the opportunities inherent in celebrating and promoting this multicultural paradigm will succeed; those that remain exclusive will not. Your leadership is the determining factor.

Our call to action is that corporations, non-profits, and governmental organizations seek to be relevant as demographics continue to evolve. Latinos and Latinas are quickly becoming a market force in the United States, as their buying power is increasing from $212 billion in 1990 to a projected $1.3 trillion in 2013. That's an increase of 554 percent—higher than the growth rate of any other racial or ethnic group (Humphreys, 2008). The Pew Hispanic Center (2009) reports that Latinas are joining the labor force at about the same rates as other American women, and yet they remain severely under-represented at the middle- and upper-management levels. With just one Latina on the board of a Fortune 100 company, it is apparent that American companies and organizations are not taking full advantage of the opportunities that American Latinas represent. Their biculturalism and bilingualism make them natural emissaries to various populations both nationally and internationally, and their loyalty makes them invaluable to companies that earn their trust and respect.

As the Latino population in the United States approaches 20 percent within the next decade, successful organizations must learn not only how to appeal to Latinos and Latinas as consumers, but also how to develop and advance them in the workplace.

In order to support these efforts, Fortune 500 companies, institutions, government, and non-profit entities can benefit from the rapidly growing multicultural, highly educated and high performing Latino and Latina professionals.

Highlights

+ Latinos will account for 45 percent of total population growth in the United States between 2003 and 2013. By 2016, the Latino labor force is expected to exceed 26 million.
+ Hispanics in the U.S., are projected to have buying power of $1.3 trillion by 2013.

- Engaging Latinos, as consumers and as organizational leaders, is essential to bottom-line success because they can bring diverse viewpoints, fresh ideas, and the "Latino lens" to business decisions.

- Latinos are not homogeneous, but represent diverse cultures of many different countries.

- Barriers to the upward mobility of Latino employees include navigating corporate politics, a lack of role models, and misconceptions about Latino culture.

- Latinas are severely under-represented in middle- and upper- level management positions in American companies, even though they are joining the labor force at about the same rates as other American women.

- An important step for corporations and non-profit organizations, is to support immigration reform.

Preface

TODAY is July 4th, Independence Day. It was my Puerto Rican father's favorite holiday. Rafael Benitez was a retired Admiral in the U.S. Navy and a passionate patriot. As a child, I remember we always hoisted the American flag outside our home and commemorated the day listening to "Pop" read the Declaration of Independence. As I got older, I recall attending the citizenship ceremonies conducted, under a tent, in the broiling heat at Bayfront Park in Miami. I was deeply touched to see hundreds of people becoming new American citizens and singing the national anthem.

The infusion and inclusion of this new group of people is the backbone of the United States. They are our future leaders. It is hope that brings them to America and it's their promise to work and grow that makes this country great. *Latinization and the Latino Leader,* salutes these courageous people. Marlene González and I, Cristina Benitez, created this book to help companies develop, retain, and advance Latinos in the workforce. Today more than ever, this is possible because of dynamic changes taking place in our world.

A re-ordered world

A confluence of events in the second decade of the 21st century created a new paradigm for Latinos in the United States. Since the turn of the century, the United States witnessed a new U.S. Census 2010, Arizona SB 1070, skyrocketing unemployment, economic implosion, natural resources explosion, diversity growth, and majority decline, and the first bi-racial American President.

Is the picture bleak? We believe not.

One of the most positive and visible changes in the next forty years will be the population growth of Latinos and the Latinization of the United States. Companies will expand market share by targeting Latinos, employers will recruit, train and develop Latino talent, political constituencies will seek talented public servants, and universities will develop curriculum to prepare students to engage with Latinos as citizens.

The massive, at times unexpected, convergence of factors noted above pave the way for a new world order for Latino leaders and their influence on the U.S. A number of positive forces support the impact of the rise of Latino leaders including three salient factors: the speed of technology, the evolution of acculturation, and a move toward immigration reform.

Technology and a shared world space

The extraordinary speed of telecommunications provides the ability to see multiple world-views simultaneously. The birth of social media, twitter, blogs, webinars and Skype allow for a convergence of cultures, languages, customs and behaviors. Globalization is breaking down international barriers and shaping a shared world space. As humans our behavior is changing because the cultural conditions surrounding us are changing. The new world order is about shared cultural values and an acceptance of diversity unknown in previous immigration patterns. Previously the new arrivals assimilated into the mainstream culture as much as possible to the point of changing their names to anglicized versions—Juan became John.

One of the most overt examples of this change is the increase in biracial marriages. According to a Pew Research Study released in June 2010, one in seven new marriages in 2008 were interracial or interethnic. This is the highest percentage in U.S. history. Interracial marriages have soared since the 1980s. In the 1980s approximately seven percent of newly married couples reported marrying outside their race or ethnicity. That number nearly doubled to approximately fifteen percent in the recent Pew report, which surveyed newlyweds in 2008. The Millennial generation demonstrates this change because they have grown up in a multicultural world and see or rather don't "see" the differences as overtly as previous generations. From the time they were born many Millennials have seen their world as multilingual, multicolored, and multi-cultured.

A new view of acculturation

In the past demographers, marketers, and social scientists calculated an immigrant's level of acculturation (the degree by which a newcomer accepts, adapts and embraces a new host culture) by a variety of factors. They included the length of residency in the new host country, language preference in and out of home, amount of television consumed in the newcomer's native language, educational level, and household income.

Because of the new world order described above, these parameters are too limiting. Instead we are looking at the immigrant's change in behavior in different circumstances. Does the immigrant maintain traditional behavior patterns relative to religious practices, dating, marriage and family, food preparation, time life balance, and his relationship to time? Will this new citizen abandon his native language to learn and speak only English as his grandparents were forced to do? The answer is no!

Marta Insua, VP Strategic Insights at Alma DDB, spearheaded an eight-month study released in 2009 entitled *The Brave New World of Consumidores*. The title conveys the mixture or fusion of cultures and languages because it mixes English and Spanish. This report identifies four levels of acculturation: Preservers, Fusionistas, American Embracers, and Eclectic Selectors, which will be discussed in depth in Chapter 2. What makes these denominations interesting is that they are based on the person's behavior and how it adapts in different circumstances. The most adaptable is the Fusionista, because this person navigates and cultivates both his native culture as well as his new American culture seamlessly. This is the sector that is producing the new Latino leader.

Immigration reform NOW!

Immigration reform is a high priority and has been for a number of Presidential administrations. However it is pushed to the back of the demonstration line because of unforeseen events such as 9/11, Katrina, the economic crisis, wars, the BP oil spill in the Gulf of Mexico, along with other unpredictable issues. Many legislators have taken up the fight, including the late Edward Kennedy, Luis Gutierrez, Dick Durbin, Charles Schumer, and Lindsey Graham, but the system remains broken and people are getting impatient.

In April 2010, Arizona Governor Jan Brewer signed SB 1070, "Support Our Law Enforcement and Safe Neighborhoods Act." The act makes it a misdemeanor in Arizona for an immigrant to be there without carrying registration documents required by federal law. Moreover, SB 1070 authorizes state and local law enforcement of federal immigration laws, and punishes those sheltering, hiring, and transporting undocumented people. Many say SB 1070 encourages racial profiling, which has resulted in demonstrations and the exodus of immigrants from Arizona. The law was modified by Arizona House Bill 2162 within a week of its signing with the goal of addressing some of these concerns. It was scheduled to go into effect on July 29, 2010, but the day before, a federal judge blocked the most controversial part that called for police officers to check a person's immigration status.

The issue is complex because it not only affects the people who come into the U.S. illegally, but also their innocent children who grow up here. It is complicated because America needs the labor most immigrants bring to this country. It fosters fear because it marginalizes people. It is not in tune with the new world order.

In a pre-July 4th speech, President Barak Obama addressed American University students and faculty on the subject of immigration reform. His remarks included, ". . . the tensions around immigration are not new. We've always defined ourselves as a nation of immigrants—a nation that welcomes those willing to embrace America's precepts. Indeed, it is this constant flow of immigrants that helped to make America what it is. But, the system is broken. And everybody knows it. Unfortunately, reform has been held hostage to political posturing and special-interest wrangling—and to the pervasive sentiment in Washington that tackling such a thorny and emotional issue is inherently bad politics."

If you have read this much of *Latinization and the Latino Leader*, you are vested in the immigration issue and we urge you to push for reform.

The book is organized to prepare and assist companies and organizations in developing their growing talent pool of Latino leaders.

Chapter 1—The Latinization Explosion

Sets the stage for the increased Latino influences in the U.S. It discusses the diversity of Latinos and provides Latino cultural themes and values to help organizations understand their Latino leaders.

Chapter 2—Making Sense of the Census

Provides the most recent statistical data and projections for the U.S. Latino population. It also provides information on Latinos' financial impact and how it is changing. This chapter explores the Latino consumer and takes a close look at segmentation providing organizations a richer understanding of how to connect with this diverse target market.

Chapter 3—The Emerging Latino Leader

Examines the present and projected impact of the U.S. Latino labor force, defines the most common challenges emerging Latino leaders face in the workplace, and offers valuable insights from *The Emerging Latino Leader: Attitudes and Behaviors in the Workplace* study. This original study included 100 Latino leaders in mid- to senior-level positions. The study looked at "The Latino professional," personality traits, preferred leadership style, and how the Latino cultural context influences factors such as leadership success, derailments, and competence.

Chapter 4—A Narrow Pipeline for Latinos

Investigates Latino employees' representation at major corporations and gives organizations tangible solutions to successfully develop, retain, and advance Latino leaders.

Chapter 5—Breaking the Glass Ceiling

Explores the existing barriers to Latino advancement, such as bias, stereotyping, and corporate politics. It tackles the glass ceiling and looks at diversity and inclusion. This chapter addresses ways to help Latino employees take responsibility and direct their careers.

Chapter 6—The Latino Leadership Competency Model

Introduces the Latino competency model, developed by the authors especially for this work. It is a unique view of the archetypes that influence Latino cultural values and the key competencies these values bring to organizations.

Chapter 7—The Power of Networking and Mentoring

Introduces concrete ways to expand Latino employees' networking capabilities, discusses the platforms organizations can use to enhance their networking infrastructure, and details a mentoring strategy program designed to connect emerging leaders with senior executives.

Chapter 8—MyBrand and Having a Voice at the Table

Creates *MyBrand*, an innovative approach to helping employees assess their individual strengths, weaknesses, and talents. In a world bombarded by information, choices, and competition, it is important to define one's personal "brand" to confidently promote oneself throughout the organization and community.

Chapter 9—Latinas as Professional Leaders

Examines the growth, vitality and future of Latinas as leaders. Three outstanding Latina leaders share their stories of how they rose to the top of their professions and provide concrete examples of what it took. This chapter delves deeper into our proprietary study. We conducted further investigation by partnering with the National Hispana Leadership Institute in a new proprietary study, Latinas as Corporate Leaders, that surveyed 250 Latina professionals to help organizations understand and better use their Latino talent.

Latinization and the Latino Leader was created to empower companies and enhance business' practices for the development, retention, and advancement of Latino employees at every level. Like most books, this work contains the authors' hopes, dreams, and our personal commitment to developing Latino talent in this country. It seems fitting that as I write this introduction I witnessed an African-American family walking down the street with their matching July 4th Family reunion t-shirts, an Indian restaurant giving away appetizers from a linen-covered table in front of its business, and a Latino family with coolers, music boxes, grandmother and kids heading to the beach. This afternoon there will be a Fourth of July celebration with actors dressed as Thomas Jefferson, Ben Franklin, and Uncle Sam leading a multigenerational, multicultural gathering of people honoring the freedom and country we pay tribute to today.

—CRISTINA BENITEZ
JULY 4, 2010

CHAPTER 1

The Latinization Explosion

SONIA SOTOMAYOR, Supreme Court justice; José Hernandez, astronaut; Gustavo Dudamel, conductor, Los Angeles Philharmonic: Latino leaders are breaking barriers and making a difference. From 1990 to 2000, the United States witnessed an unprecedented 60 percent growth in the Latino population from all parts of Latin America and by Latinos born in the United States. The 2010 Census is projected to show similar increases. The twenty-first century has ushered in a global perspective that is aiming at being more inclusive, and the Latino explosion is leading the way. If you are a business looking to hire, develop, and retain Latinos, or if you are a Latino leader, your time has come.

> "Our greatness as a nation has depended on individual initiative . . . but it has also depended on our sense of mutual regard for each other, of mutual responsibility. The idea that everybody has a stake in the country, that we're all in this together and everybody's got a shot at opportunity—Americans know this."
>
> —Barack Obama, August 7, 2006

What is Latinization?

Latinization is mainstream America's adoption and acceptance of Latino culture, customs, and values. Salsa, the tango, and tortillas are just a few examples of how Latino culture has been embraced by the general population in areas such as food, music, language, and work ethic. This acceptance of Latino culture is giving Latinos the latitude to be more authentic and accepted in the workplace.

Though it is a stretch to say that everyone regards Latinos favorably, there is a greater willingness to be open to Latinos than in the past. As a result, they are more likely to express the importance of their culture, values, and customs. They can retain Spanish names and share aspects of their culture in the workplace. Depending on the corporate culture, Latinos can express their cultural heritage and live authentically in the workplace rather than have one persona for work and another for home.

Although many Latinos are not native Spanish speakers, many are. Yet there are still companies that forbid Spanish in the workplace. Today, more companies accept Spanish-speaking in the workplace, and numerous businesses offer Spanish classes because their leadership realizes it is a valuable workforce skill. While Latinos are feeling more at ease living their Latino authenticity, they are also adapting to the mainstream culture as many bicultural/bilingual Latinos do today, and this helps them maneuver and succeed in business.

Understanding Latinization

Latinos can retain much of their culture due to the number of Hispanics living in the U.S., the infrastructure supporting them, and a new acceptance of diversity ushered in with the Obama era.

Historically, an immigrant who lived in this country long enough eventually left his traditions behind to embrace American culture. Today because of communication, travel, media, and the Internet, the adaptation is taking on new dimensions. When a new culture is introduced into a host culture, each culture will inevitably affect and influence the other in a process known as interacculturation. The result is a constantly evolving mainstream society that is fueled by interconnected cultures. In the case of Latino culture, this is called Latinization or Hispanization. Today, the process of Latinization is taking place in nearly every aspect of life in the United States including social, health, politics, entertainment, manufacturing, the arts, business, and the corporate world.

The future of Latinization

The increasing Latino population, coupled with the Obama era, has ushered in an expanded view of race and ethnicity. Inclusion is part of the life experience of Generation Xers (born between 1965 and 1976), Millennials (born between 1977 and 1994), and the Matrix Generation (born from 1994 to present).

In 2010 nearly 48 percent of Latinos were under age 35, and age influences the way a person perceives racial and cultural interaction. These Latinos as well as the rest of mainstream America have grown up in multicultural classrooms. Those who are Latino, Asian, or African American don't necessarily see themselves as minorities and have friends from all backgrounds. This inclusiveness gives them the freedom to express their unique cultures and languages.

These are the leaders of today and tomorrow. Latinos will increasingly add to the ranks, and Latinization will empower them to incorporate Latino values in conference rooms, sales calls, team meetings, and corporate board appointments.

Understanding that your Latino employee represents a fraction of the Latino population means you know which country he is from; but digging deeper, where in that country is he from, what city or town? Is he from a city such as Mexico City, a metropolis of 20 million, or Juncos, Puerto Rico, with the much smaller population of 36,500. Or did he grow up in El Paso, Texas, an American city whose Hispanic density is 82 percent? You should know how long he has lived in the U.S., or if native born, his acculturation level. This affects his attitude toward the importance of his Latino heritage and how both he and you can use Latino values to improve productivity, results, and career advancement.

A Pew Hispanic Center report released in late 2009 defines the top 10 countries of origin for Latinos who live in the United States as Mexico, Puerto Rico, Cuba, El Salvador, Dominican Republic, Guatemala, Colombia, Honduras, Ecuador, and Peru. Figures 1.1 and 1.2 detail the U.S. Latino population from the these countries. Although approximately 65 percent of the U.S. Latino population is of Mexican origin, it is important to understand that Mexican culture is not homogeneous. Regional differences in food, history, music, traditions, geography, and even language reflect the diversity of Mexico.

Every culture has its own particular social constructs and mores that influence the people who come from that culture. For example, social constructs in Cuba and Puerto Rico encourage outspokenness; Latinos from other places with more prominent indigenous populations, such as Mexico and Central America, may not be perceived as assertive. Understanding your Latino leader's origins pays off in better communication due to cultural awareness.

Graciela Fernandez is an excellent example of this. Graciela is from Guatemala with strong Mayan influence in her ancestry. She began her career as an entry-level receptionist in a telecommunications company in 2006. She was polite and quick to do her job, but her shy nature kept her from advancement until she found a mentor who coached her on the importance of speaking up and being forthright with her ideas. With this training she was assigned to an additional project, and though it was awkward for Graciela, she pushed herself to share her ideas. At the end of 2008, Graciela was promoted to manager of customer engagement for a new product scheduled to launch in 2009. When the economy faltered, the project was shelved, but Graciela was retained, and in spite of layoffs, Graciela is still working.

Figure 1.1　The ten largest Latino population groups in the United States by country of origin, 2008

(based on self-described family ancestry or place of birth)

All Hispanics	**46,822,000**
Mexicans	30, 746,00
Puerto Ricans	4,151,000
Cubans	1,631,000
Salvadorans	1,560,000
Dominicans	1,334,000
Guatemalans	986,000
Colombians	882,000
Hondurans	608,000
Ecuadorians	591,000
Peruvians	519,000

Source: Pew Hispanic Center

Figure 1.2 Percent of Hispanics who are U.S. citizens, by country of origin

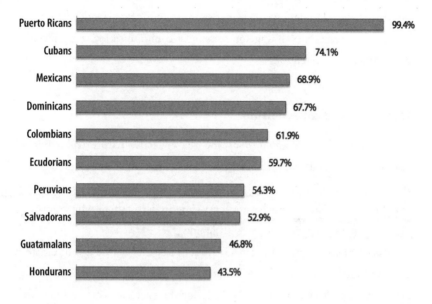

Puerto Ricans	99.4%
Cubans	74.1%
Mexicans	68.9%
Dominicans	67.7%
Colombians	61.9%
Ecudorians	59.7%
Peruvians	54.3%
Salvadorans	52.9%
Guatamalans	46.8%
Hondurans	43.5%

Source: Pew Hispanic Center

Heart and soul: Latino values

Unless you've had the opportunity to live abroad for an extended period or have spent time living in a high-density Latino barrio of the United States, it is difficult for non-Latinos to really grasp Latino values. Cultural patterns are learned by spending time with people in day-to-day activities. How do people celebrate birthdays, holidays, and family gatherings? What is the interaction between generations and siblings? What principles do they hold dear, that serve as the framework for building character? Understanding these nuances takes time, interest, and travel to Latin America or to the Latino neighborhoods in the United States. Taking the time to ask these questions and absorb the answers is imperative. By understanding Latinos' history and appreciating their cultural treasures, by listening to their music and seeing their art, you can further your understanding of Latino cultural values.

Some of the values Latinos cherish are family, loyalty, trust, respect, a diligent work ethic, and passion. Understanding the various dynamics and levels on which cultural values operate provides an authentic framework that informs and guides strategic planning for consumer communication and employee development and retention.

Familismo and collectivismo

The concept of family (*familismo*) and the collective nature (*collectivismo*) Latino families hold dear may be difficult for mainstream companies to understand. Whereas U.S. culture encourages independence, Latinos yearn for the togetherness of family and have a hard time understanding why companies don't recognize their need to be with family.

Rafael Siquieros moved from Guayaquil, Ecuador at the age of eighteen to attend university in the United States. He has been a middle management employee at a national utilities company for the past ten years and has hit a plateau professionally, feeling he is being passed over for promotion. Rafael had an opportunity to relocate and get a better position in the company, but that was not an option for him, especially at this time.

Over the past ten years, Rafael moved his family (his mother, father, brother, and two sisters) to live with him and made room in his large home to accommodate the family. When I asked Rafael about his family, he pulled out a worn photo from his wallet that showed the entire clan, including his wife and two children. He smiled broadly; his demeanor softened, and he said, "I am so glad to have them living with me. We are all together now." Is it crowded? Yes, but having his family together is a primary value. Knowing that his mother and father, his children's grandparents, are there to be part of his children's lives means more to him than having more space. He knows that his brothers and sisters will eventually move on, but for now, having the family close is what truly matters. Moreover, when other family members come for the holidays, Rafael and his family always find a place for them to stay in his home, even if it is on the couch or temporary mattress.

The Spanish saying *de rincón al rincón todo un colchón* literally translates as "from corner to corner, the whole room is a mattress." It means that Latinos like, want, and need to have their families close. Families spending time together is a treasured value.

The importance of family cannot be stressed enough. Joxel illustrates another example. Joxel García was born and raised in Puerto Rico. He graduated from Ponce School of Medicine, in Ponce, Puerto Rico, and did his residency in obstetrics and gynecology at Mount Sinai Hospital in Hartford, Connecticut. He is an American physician and former four-star admiral in the U.S. Public Health Service Commissioned Corps. At the age 46, Admiral García served from March 13, 2008 to January 20, 2009 as the thirteenth Assistant Secretary for Health (ASH) at the U.S. Department of Health and Human Services. He currently serves as the president of the Ponce School of Medicine. In an interview with Raymond J. Arroyo that was published in *The Business Journal of Hispanic Research* (a publication of the National Society of Hispanic MBAs), Dr. García discussed leadership and his thoughts regarding professional and personal success:

> *"If people look at my professional career and personal accomplishments, they may consider me successful; however, I cannot consider myself successful because I have significant lessons to learn still. In addition, I want to be the best father that I can be to my two children. I want to better guide them and protect them. To me, success at the personal level is much more important than professional success . . . until I have contributed to creating the best family that I can and see my two young children secure a bright, independent future, and I have conveyed to them in no uncertain terms how much they mean to me."*

Power of the group

Latino culture is one of relationships, social interaction, and verbal exchange. This is seen in the workplace, and it tends to be more visceral when Latinos congregate together because physicality is a part of their culture. Latinos simply have more body contact, such as cheek kissing, touching arms, and so forth. Although this may not be politically correct in today's work environment, this behavior is what Latinos grow up with; it's comfortable for them. They recognize that they need to hold back at work. Conversely, the idea of being in a group that works together to solve problems does feel comfortable. Collectivism is the basis of collaboration. The ability to work and relate in groups has been shown to increase creative problem solving and innovation. In his book *Group Genius: The Creative Power of Collaboration*, Keith Sawyer discusses the benefits of group work. Says Sawyer, "When we collaborate, creativity unfolds, across people; sparks fly faster, and the whole is greater than the sum of its parts." Collaboration is a natural construct for Latinos. They prefer being in groups, and companies can capitalize on this natural value and use it to spark ideas.

Respect, trust, loyalty, and passion

Other values such as respect, trust, and loyalty all stem from *familismo*. Respect for parents and the elderly is undisputable. Children are taught unconditional respect in the form of politeness and deference to parents and grandparents. This is reflected in the way they speak to elders, peers, and the younger generation. Rather than confront others, they want to hear them out and politely respond. As Latinos mature, they traditionally pass this respect on to people of authority and high professional stature. In today's business climate sullied by greed, deception, and failing businesses, this is changing, but respect still remains a strong value for many. Latinos also derive valuable respect from a job well done. Working hard to accomplish tasks is a source of respect and dignity for Latino employees.

For Latinos, trust and loyalty are also values derived from *familismo*. We know we can trust our families because they demonstrate they are present in our lives and we can count on them. Trust in the workplace does not come automatically. Knowing you can count on or *contar con* someone after they've fulfilled their responsibility develops trust and, in turn, loyalty. Latinos are known for their loyalty; they believe in it when trust is there, and this makes for a committed employee.

Passion—the outward expression of enthusiasm, energy, or spirit—is a Latino characteristic seen for better or worse in the workplace. For some non-Latinos, passion has the connotation of being out of control or overly dramatic, which can be inappropriate in a work setting. It's not uncommon to see a group of Latinos in the company cafeteria being more animated because of its social context, and they are more likely to show emotions in that social setting than if they are in the boardroom. Passion is one characteristic that may make your Latino employee stand out and appear different but as Chief Diversity Officer at Hewitt Associates, Andrés Tapia, states in his book *The Inclusion Paradox*, in calling out the differences, different modes of expression can be minimized and ameliorated.

Summary

The concept of emotional intelligence (EI), a term coined by Daniel Goleman, describes the ability to discern and engage with one's own and others' emotions to guide one's thinking and actions. Bringing the values of compassion, respect, enthusiasm, empathy, self-awareness, and humanity to work and ultimately connecting with others at a deep level results in stronger, more productive leadership. These values are inherent in Latino culture's emphasis on *familismo* and *collectivismo*. According to Goleman, we depend on our relationships with others for our own emotional stability. In the previous example of Dr. García, he demonstrates that having a high IQ is certainly important, but EI is equally crucial to being a strong leader.

The increased size and projected growth of Latinos coupled with the Latinization of mainstream culture opens the doors for the twenty-first century Latino. As the United States continues to incorporate Latino food, music, art, literature, and other cultural products into mainstream culture, Latinization provides the framework for the inclusion of Latino employees. These bicultural, bilingual employees with ties to both cultures bring measurable values to a business world that is struggling today.

Your Latino employee is the future of business. An intimate knowledge of Latinos means the company practices inclusion and welcomes new ideas that spring from differences. An intimate knowledge provides a framework to acknowledge and motivate people to contribute their best, and that is what all companies seek.

CHAPTER 2

Making Sense of the Census and Latino Consumers

THE 2000 Census was an eye-opener. Many were surprised to learn that the Latino population had become the largest ethnic group in the U.S., accounting for over 15 percent of the population. Major entry points, the cities where the majority of Latinos lived such as Los Angeles, New York, Miami, Chicago, and Houston, maintained their relative positions as the cities with the largest Latino populations. However, during the past ten years, Latinos began moving into nearly all states and away from metropolitan areas into smaller towns and neighborhoods. This shift in population has major implications for businesses, corporations, and other organizations that employ Latinos and seek to engage Latino consumers.

The changing numbers

According to the U.S. Census Bureau, the Latino population is projected to grow almost 36 percent from 2005 to 2015 to nearly 58 million, compared with almost 6 percent growth for non-Latinos in the same period. Children are a big part of the story and since 2000, babies born in the U.S. to Latino parents increased by 3 percent, while non-Hispanic births declined 20 percent. Today, one quarter of all the nation's babies are Hispanic!

It is important to note that Latinos are not a racial group; instead, they are an ethnic group. As seen below, Latinos can be black, white, Indian, Asian, or a mixture of many races. The 2000 Census was the first to ask citizens if they were a mixture of ethnicities and race; the 2010 Census will no doubt paint a picture of a multiracial society.

Figure 2.1   Comparison of population by race and Latino origin

	2003		2008 (est.)		2013 (proj.)		% change	% change
	number	%	number	%	number	%	2003–08	2008–13
Race								
Asian	11,933	4.1	13,742	4.5	15,669	4.9	15.2	14.0
Black	37,082	12.7	39,210	12.9	41,237	12.9	5.7	5.2
White	234,241	80.5	242,995	79.8	252,386	79.0	3.7	3.9
Other*	7,594	2.6	8,536	2.8	10,038	3.1	12.4	17.6
Hispanic origin								
Hispanic	39,935	13.7	46,976	15.4	54,440	17.0	17.6	15.9
Non-Hispanic	250,915	86.3	257,507	84.6	264,890	83.0	2.6	2.9
Total	290,850	100.0	304,483	100.0	319,330	100.0	4.7	4.9

*Includes American Indian/Alaska native, native Hawaiian/other Pacific Islander, and two or more races. Data may not equal totals because of rounding. Latinos can be of any race.

Source: U.S. Census Bureau, interim population projections 2008, and annual July 1 population estimates

Historically, Latinos have settled in major metropolitan cities. The top five cities—Los Angeles, New York, Miami, Chicago, and Houston—have held the lead for the past twenty years. Some Latinos stay in these urban settings, but a significant number move to outlying areas or suburbs. In fact, from 2000 to 2007, Wapelo County, Iowa witnessed a 200 percent growth rate and Shannon County, South Dakota saw a 257 percent increase in their Latino populations.

Figure 2.2   Top Ten Metropolitan Areas, 2006

Metropolitan statistical area	Total (In 000s)
Los Angeles–Long Beach–Santa Ana, CA	5,694
New York–Northern New Jersey–Long Island, NY–NJ–PA	3,985
Miami–Fort Lauderdale–Miami Beach, FL	2,093
Chicago–Naperville–Joliet, IL–IN–WI	1,829

Metropolitan statistical area	Total (In 000s)
Houston–Sugar Land–Baytown, TX	1,822
Riverside–San Bernardino–Ontario, CA	1,775
Dallas–Fort Worth–Arlington, TX	1,591
Phoenix–Mesa–Scottsdale, AZ	1,210
San Antonio, TX	1,026
San Diego–Carlsbad–San Marcos, CA	885

Source: U.S. Census Bureau, American Community Survey 2006

As companies plan, they should look at the top 10 states with the greatest percentage increase of Latino population from 2000 through 2006. In the past, California, New York, Florida and Texas were the hot spots, but today's growth is in the southern states.

Figure 2.3   States with greatest Latino population growth, 2000-2006

	2000	2006	Change 2000–06	Percent change 2000–06
Arkansas	85,303	144,394	59,091	69.3
Tennessee	116,692	187,761	71,069	60.9
Georgia	434,375	695,521	261,146	60.1
South Carolina	94,652	149,931	55,279	58.4
North Carolina	377,084	595,376	218,292	57.9
Nevada	393,397	605,059	211,662	53.8
Alabama	72,152	109,325	37,173	51.5
Iowa	80,204	120,091	39,887	49.7
Maryland	230,992	341,261	110,269	47.7
Delaware	37,811	55,572	17,761	47.0

Source: U.S. Census Bureau, American Community Survey 2006

Financial impact

According to the Selig Center for Economic Growth at the University of Georgia, Latinos are projected to reach a purchasing power of $1.3 trillion by 2013. The Selig Center states that Latino purchasing power is growing at higher rates than other ethnic and racial groups and the general population.

The Selig Center reports that the number of Latinos who earned $100,000 and had at least $500,000 in assets was growing eight times faster than for non-Latinos. Much of this can be attributed to Latino's increasing levels of educational attainment, English-language proficiency, and career development.

Latino household income is also growing. In 2007, the Tomás Rivera Policy Institute reported the number of Latino households earning more than $100,000 annually grew 126 percent from 1991 through 2000, compared with 77 percent for the general population.

Contribution to Gross Domestic Product

In December 2009, the Fiscal Policy Institute Immigration Research Initiative released a new study, *Immigrants and the Economy*. The research reports on Latinos' contributions to the gross domestic product (GDP) and examines the economic role of immigrants in the 25 largest metropolitan areas in the United States. It reports strong immigrant contribution to GDP, and it is the first report that estimates immigrant share of gross domestic product in metro areas, based on wage and salary earnings plus proprietors' income.

The median age of the Latino population is around 27 years, which places the majority of Latinos in the U.S. in the active working ages. Immigrants work in a wide range of jobs from lower-wage service or blue-collar occupations to higher-paying jobs. With 49 percent of Latino workers in the first two categories, the potential to develop Latino leaders is clear.

- 24 percent work in managerial and professional occupations
- 25 percent work in technical, sales, and administrative support
- 23 percent work in service occupations
- 27 percent work in blue-collar occupations

Totals don't equal 100 because of geographical differences

Two-thirds of all immigrants live in the 25 largest metropolitan areas. The combined income of foreign-born workers in these areas contributes 20 percent of the economic input and they make up 20 percent of the population.

This pattern holds true, with slight variation, for each of the 25 areas, from metro Pittsburgh, where immigrants represent 3 percent of population and 4 percent of GDP, to metro Miami, where immigrants make up 37 percent of the population and 38 percent of GDP.

2010 Census

As this book goes to press, we are on the threshold of the release of results from the 2010 Census. The U.S. Census Bureau will report the results in March 2011; the magnitude of data collected will have a profound influence on our lives. It will determine each state's congressional representation and affect more than $400 billion in annual state and federal funds allocated to local communities for improvements in education, public health, new roads, job training centers, services for the elderly, and more.

The state and federal funding amounts to $30 trillion dollars over a 10-year period. One of the most important facts to be revealed by the census is the expected increase in immigration and where these new inhabitants live. City planners will study the effects of immigration on every aspect of our lives.

The Pew Hispanic Center has a useful interactive map of 3,141 counties in the U.S. that shows the population density, percentage of Latinos, and growth of Latinos from 1980 to 2007. It also demonstrates which counties are experiencing the fastest growth in Latino population. This tool is a comprehensive overview of the Latino population as determined by the U.S. census, and until the 2010 numbers are tallied, it serves as an accessible resource for understanding the size and growth of this population.

Impact of 2010 Census on media & Latino consumers

Telemundo Communications Group president Don Browne has no doubt the 2010 Census will be "a game-changer" for Hispanics. In an interview during the Hispanic TV Summit 2009, Browne remarked that Latinos and the media that serve them should expect big things after the 2010 numbers are tallied.

Although marketers are aware that large numbers of Hispanics reside in New York, Los Angeles, Houston, Chicago, and Miami, "post-census" data will detail exactly where members of the largest and fastest-growing ethnic minority in the U.S. live. Browne noted for those "who have not had a wake-up call, this is going to put us over the top."

Latinization and acculturation

In the past, Latinos have been expected, and sometimes required, to blend into the mainstream; but today, Latinos can retain and even celebrate their heritage. No longer is it necessary to go through the process of assimilation whereby immigrants had to give up all their traditional values. Latinos have replaced assimilation with varying degrees of acculturation, which allows them to retain their culture and language. Acculturation today is an on-going process that is a continuous blending of cultures creating the multicultural population of the 21st century.

Historically, immigrants assimilated to such a degree that they even changed their names so they would sound more "American." But at today's high school and college graduation ceremonies, you will hear a list of names from all over the globe. This demonstrates the growing trend in acculturation to maintain native culture. In the 2009 Springfield Illinois High School's graduation class, the list of graduates reflected the multicultural mix of today's youth with names such as Zack Gardner, Sohaib Ahmed, Sharon Kim, Sanum Zaidi, and Maria Consuela Castillo.

How much of an immigrant's native culture is retained is a complex and multilayered issue, and a person's age and origin of birth are significant factors. Older Latinos rely more heavily on traditional roles, whereas young Latinos create an interesting interplay of history, cultural traditions, and contemporary mores. The Latinization of the U.S., the increasing influence of Latinos on mainstream culture and your consumer, is one social construct that has evolved from the trend toward acculturation.

A glimpse at your customer

This chapter has outlined the size, growth, and financial impact of Latinos in the U.S. These impact your bottom line as they relate to your consumer. As the non-Latino population and market share decline, Hispanic consumer opportunities increase. Most major corporations have had significant Hispanic marketing initiatives for twenty years or more. In 1996, the Association of Hispanic Advertising Agencies (AHAA) was founded as a trade organization to support, govern, conduct research, and foster growth for the Hispanic advertising industry. It is important to understand that the Hispanic consumer target is more than a number; it is more than a Spanish-speaking target, but a multifaceted segment that needs to be viewed from the standpoint of cultural relevancy and lifestyle choice.

Slicing the pie

There are many ways to segment the Hispanic target market. Length of residency in the U.S., nationality, age, language preference, acculturation level, and consumer attitudes and behaviors are all factored into segmentation. Segmenting the Hispanic target market is increasingly complex, yet it provides the opportunity to focus messaging on the Latino employee or target consumer and communicate in a way that resonates on a cultural and emotional level.

In July 2010, Viacom Inc. released a new ad for its bicultural cable TV station Tr3s. You see a Latino at the grocery store and as each item from

macaroni and cheese to *plátanos* and sushi are scanned a voice authorizes the product in the appropriate language. It even differentiates between Caribbean and Mexican food. It is a clever way of recognizing today's multicultural U.S. society. The tagline is: *Two cultures—one channel.*

This ad highlights a Hispanic marketing trend toward the acculturated, bilingual, bicultural Latino that some are calling *Fusionistas.* In a yellow paper released in Fall 2009, Marta Insua, vice president of strategic insights at advertising agency Alma DDB, used the term "Fusionista" to identify this segment that is mostly U.S. born and English oriented, but also speaks Spanish as an indication of his dual Anglo/Latino cultural identity.

Figure 2.4   Slicing the pie

28% Fusionistas:
  Much more than the
  best of both worlds

20% American Embracers:
  Keep belonging simple

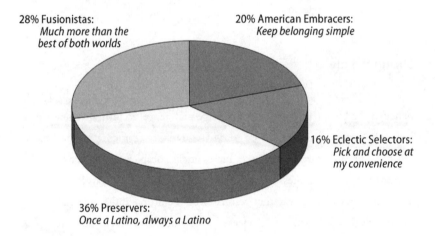

16% Eclectic Selectors:
  Pick and choose at
  my convenience

36% Preservers:
  Once a Latino, always a Latino

Source: A Brave New World of Consumidores—Introducing Fusionistas, *a yellow paper from Alma DDB,*
September 2009.

Fusionistas see themselves as having the best of both worlds. Fusionistas are distinguished from the "Preservers" who are foreign born, prefer Spanish, and cling to the traditional Latino cultural lifestyle. At the other end of the spectrum are the "American Embracers" who are mostly U.S. born, predominantly English speaking, and identify with the general market or the Anglo lifestyle. To identify these categories, Alma DDB created the Cultural Curators Unit to research the key demographics of these young (18-to-34-year-old) bicultural Latinos.

Why does this matter?

What does this mean to companies seeking to understand their Latino employees? Interesting comparisons can be made about how best to communicate with the Latino employees' different acculturation levels.

The following chart is from the Alma DDB report and describes four acculturation segments that apply to Latinos. It can serve for advertising as well as understanding the Latino employee. Where do your new hires or existing employees line up? Are they more comfortable in Spanish, English, or the combination of both known as "Spanglish." Do they live in a Latino or Anglo culture, or are they relaxed in, comfortable in, and celebratory of both?

Figure 2.5   Hispanic Marketing Trend on Acculturation

Preservers 36%	Fusionistas 28%	Eclectic Selectors 16%	American Embracers 20%
Spanish oriented	English oriented	Spanish oriented	English dominant
High cultural affinity	Dual cultural affinity	Low cultural affinity	Low Hispanic affinity
Retain most of Hispanic culture and family values	Ties with both cultures: Hispanic affinity as intense as Preserves	Spanish dominant	English dominant
More comfortable with and prefer Spanish		Seek fast Anglo acculturation	Fully adopted Anglo culture
	English dominant but Spanish essential cultural connector	Mostly foreign born	Still self-defined Hispanics
Mostly foreign born			U.S. born
	Mostly U.S. born		

Source: Alma DDB

How to connect with Fusionistas

+ Make mastering cultural affinity a priority strategy. Walk away from the Spanish-versus-English mindset and acculturation metrics, and become obsessed with the cultural affinity lens.

+ Understand the difference between in-language and in-culture and how Spanglish and its constant evolution is used by urban youth.

+ Acknowledge Fusionistas' dual-faceted identity and values that fuse the best of both worlds. Use constructs that facilitate their expression of these, e.g., the Salsa dancing, modern Latino entrepreneur.

+ Embrace their passion for collaboration and self-expression. Don't talk "at" them; rather, provide them with channels that will foster their content generation.

+ Embrace in-culture opportunities. Fusionistas are still Latinos, but the insights into their behavior are richer and more challenging.

+ Provide all-encompassing entertainment. Fusionistas are primarily young; they do not differentiate entertainment from information from work; and they cherish their individual identity, which they express through their unique style in fashion, music, and food.

+ Engage the community through grass-roots mobilization. Understanding the role of new technology and cultivating an urban tone will help overcome limits of traditional media and provide opportunities to reach Fusionistas in a relevant manner, e.g., through social networking, mobile media, and street activism.

+ Increase education, the ultimate enabler of the achievement of the American dream and the access to the modern world. Fusionistas are determined to help their Hispanic community sort out the difficulties implicit in navigating an unfamiliar system.

Summary

Companies seeking to increase their bottom line and develop Latino leaders draw from a pool of talent that includes Latin American expatriates, candidates who have completed college and graduate degrees in the U.S., or Latinos born and educated in the U.S. The latter grew up with the American dream, and like the Fusionistas, they celebrate the cultural heritage and Latino values learned from their families in the U.S. Unlike their parents, they don't feel that speaking Spanish will hold them back; rather, it is a valuable skill in a globalized economy.

According to the *2008 American Community Survey* (ACS) from the U.S. Census Bureau, approximately 61 percent of the Latino population (28,179,000) was born in the United States. Among foreign-born Latinos, many millions are highly acculturated, which means they are fluent in English and Spanish and identify strongly with both American cultures. These employees provide the lens through which to see and understand your Latino customer. In addition to a diverse point of view, they help companies hone their communications to target the fastest-growing consumer market in the United States.

The projected growth of Latinos in this century and their advancement into leadership roles gives companies an ongoing source to increase revenue. Latino employees are valuable assets as sounding boards or as a "Latino compass" for advertising, and many companies are not using this resource. Including Latinos as part of the marketing team so they interact with your Hispanic agency provides your company with a litmus test for both the message and the product's relevance to your intended target. Your employees know your products better than anyone, and they can provide invaluable insights.

CHAPTER 3

The Emerging Latino Leader

MANY organizations recognize that Latinos leaders can contribute to corporate life in immeasurable ways. Some realize that diverse perspectives at the employee, managerial, and executive levels can bring fresh ideas, energy, and innovation. To understand and appreciate the emerging Latino leader, we first need to understand where they stand in the general labor force and some of the Latino conundrums at work.

According to the Bureau of Labor Statistics, there will be an annual growth rate in the labor force of 0.6 percent over the years 2005 through 2050, resulting in a workforce of 195 million by 2050. Prior to the economic crisis of 2008–2009, the Latino labor force was expected to grow by 30 percent to reach 27 million by 2016, whereas the non-Latino labor force was projected to grow by only 5 percent. In 2007, the Latino labor force median age was 28 years, compared with the median age of the population as a whole of 37 years. Almost 34 percent of the Latino population was younger than age 18, compared with 25 percent of the total population.

In its *Statistical Portrait of Hispanics in the United States*, the Pew Hispanic Center reported that Latinos represent 8.1 percent of the workforce in management, business, and financial operations occupations. Indeed, certain industries have relied on Latinos to grow or competitively sustain their operations.

Large numbers of young Latinos will soon be entering the labor pool. Among U.S. workers in the group aged 20 to 24, 18 percent are Latino. Valuing, developing, and advancing Latino leaders remains a tremendous challenge for businesses, as is investing in marketing campaigns to secure a piece of the Latino market share and expanding their products and services to Latin America.

The Latino leader conundrums

Why haven't Latinos made huge strides in the corporate world? Why are the numbers still low, and what are the challenges they face? Many organizations recognize that they don't have an adequate number of Latino leaders and they want to know what they can do to change this to their advantage. We address these questions when we are hired to teach organizations about Latinization.

First, it is important to understand the way in which being either "foreign born" or "U.S. born" shapes Latino leaders' perspectives and impacts their experiences within corporate culture. Pew Hispanic Center defines "foreign born" as persons born outside of the United States to parents who are not U.S. citizens. "Foreign born" also refers to those born in Puerto Rico. Although individuals born in Puerto Rico are U.S. citizens by birth, they are included among the foreign born because they are born into a predominantly Spanish culture. Their attitudes, views, and beliefs are in many ways much closer to those of Hispanics born abroad than to Latinos born in the 50 states or the District of Columbia, even those who identify themselves as being of Puerto Rican origin. "Native born" or "U.S. born" refers to persons born in the United States and those born abroad to parents at least one of whom is a U.S. citizen.

The generation to which the Latino leaders in your organization belong also determines their level of acculturation or assimilation; their level of acculturation or assimilation in turn affects their relationship with both cultures. Pew Hispanic Center employs the following definitions of first, second, third, and later generations:

First generation Latinos are foreign born, defined the same as previously;

Second generation Latinos are born in the United States and have at least one first-generation parent;

Third and later generation Latinos are born in the United States, with both parents born in the United States.

In the marketing world, this newer way of looking at acculturation, which is behavior based rather than generation based, is the more progressive of the two. Culture, religion, gender role expectations, socioeconomic factors, education level, and the degree to which Latino employees are acculturated or assimilated into the mainstream culture all contribute to the challenges Latino leaders face. Latinos working in various organizations are influenced by all of these factors to different degrees. The following are the seven most common conundrums regarding Latino leaders with which organizations should be familiar.

Between two cultures

Latinos spend their lives caught between two cultures, two identities, and in some cases, two languages. Home is where their hearts and minds were formed; work is where they aspire to be leaders. Identity issues become more complex when you take into account differences among first, second, or third generation Latinos. The first generation exhibits more Latino cultural traits and speaks Spanish as their primary language. The second generation frequently learns about Latino culture from their parents, but lives in a different social and business context and reality. The third and later generations have limited experience living the Latino culture, heritage, and traditions, and transmit little of it to their children and their cultural context.

Multilingual language capability

More than 500 million people speak Spanish, making it the third most spoken language in the world. The fourth largest Spanish-speaking population resides in the United States Bilingualism is an advantage in personal and professional growth, in social encounters, and in an educational environment. According to Synovate's *2010 U.S. Market Diversity Market Report*, at a national level, 55 percent of Latino adults speak Spanish at home, or they speak Spanish more often than English, 23 percent speak English at home, and 22 percent speak Spanish and English equally or are bilingual. But it does not provide insights into the capability of speaking either language at home. Numerous organizations discourage Latinos from speaking Spanish at work, not realizing having Spanish speakers on staff can facilitate the connection between their clients and their products or services.

Educational attainment or readiness level

As we all know, education is the great social equalizer. What is even more impressive is that Latino youths account for 5.5 million or 13 percent of the U.S. youth population according to Pew Hispanic Center. In March 2009, only 31 percent of Latino youths of appropriate age were enrolled in high school. Similarly, only 21 percent were enrolled in college. Over the years, trends of high dropout rates and low college completion rates for Latinos have widened the education gap between Latino youths and their minority peers. The reasons for dropouts among young Latinos include financial issues, the need to support their family, and poor English skills. Some say they simply dislike school and do not need more education in order to pursue the careers in which they are interested. However, of the Latinos who are enrolled in college, many attend community colleges, often only part time. Others delay or prolong their college education into their mid-20s and beyond. These findings clearly show that large numbers of Latinos try to extend their education but fail to earn a degree, which limits their ability to compete for positions of power and influence in corporate America.

Limited tenure and experience in leadership roles

Latinos are the fastest-growing segment of the labor force. They also have one of the highest rates of poverty, unemployment, and occupational segregation. Latinos tend to hold lower-paying jobs that are concentrated in nonprofessional service occupations such as gardening, cleaning , and food services. The average Latino worker is around 27 years old, compared with the average U.S. worker who is around 37 years old, which means a lack of Latino role models and limited exposure to or experience in highly visible positions or positions of power.

Limited access to networking and recruiting practices

The few Latino professionals in influential roles can act as mentors or role models to only so many aspiring Latino leaders. Up-and-coming Latinos may have less access to job openings or advancement opportunities, which are often shared through word-of-mouth or informal contacts.

Lack of interest in relocation and business travel

During the course of a normal career, relocation opportunities will likely arise. In the Latino community, providing for immediate and extended family is a priority. Many employers offer relocation assistance, such as finding schools and housing and paying for living costs. However, during the transition, this assistance extends to the employee and the employee's immediate family, not extended family. Other potential pitfalls are the lack of clarity regarding how to stay connected with the boss, team, or mentors; the lack of visibility for career advancements; and repatriation plans once the assignment is over. This is a particular challenge for Latinas who are expected to play traditional gender roles.

Challenges to traditional Latino gender roles

There are two traditional roles, *machismo* for men and *marianismo* for women. *Machismo* is a set of beliefs that contends men should be the aggressor, brave, protector, and in charge of all decisions. *Marianismo* contends that women should be submissive, obedient, grateful, faithful, poised, and honorable. Sexuality is not allowed before marriage, and to this end, Latinas are expected to live with their parents until they are married. Many first generation Latinas are expected to show servitude to their men and tend to all the household work such as cooking, cleaning, and childrearing. *Marianismo*, like *machismo*, is less relevant for second, third, and later generations of Latinos. Latinas are entering the workforce, getting educated, and demanding more of their partners than their mothers did.

The new generation: Latino Millennials

Generations, like people, have personalities, and Latino Millennials (aged 16 to 25) do not escape this trend. They are making the passage into adulthood at the start of a new millennium, especially native-born, first generation and some second generations. They are a good example of cultural fusion or what we called *Fusionistas*, and include both men and women. They are optimistic and hopeful for a better future, more educated and confident about their identity, self-expressive and communicative because they have better English capability and Spanglish. Overall they are more liberal and less religious, upbeat and open to change, and proud of their heritage. Still they embrace their American birthright. They are more ethnically and racially diverse than older Latino adults. An incredible 73 percent of Latino Millennials use social networking tools, making this generation technological savvy and socially connected. Work is considered a vehicle to life but not life itself. They are more likely than prior generations to have switched careers, already trying out different industry and fields.

The emerging Latino leader

In 2009–2010 co-author Marlene González, president of Life Coaching Group, LLC, led a study called *The Emerging Latino Leader: Attitudes and Behaviors in the Workplace*. The study examined "The Latino professional," personality traits, preferred leadership styles, and how the Latino cultural context influences factors such as leadership success, derailments, and competence.

During this process a combination of professional coaching sessions, surveys, interviews, and assessment tools were used. For personality assessments the Insights Discovery® Preference Evaluator was chosen for its validity, reliability, and accuracy. It is based on the psychological archetypes theory of Carl Jung and Jolande Jacobi and widely used for executive leadership development globally.

This process gave us the foundation to understand the dynamics of factors that influence the behavior of Latino leaders. These factors include the choice of persons on whom they model leadership and the connection between

Latino values and leadership capability. Based on the findings of this process, we developed the *Latino Leadership Competency Model* leading to a better understanding of the behavioral patterns that have an effect on Latinos' successful personal and professional lives.

The sample was comprised of 100 Latino leaders in mid-level to senior-level positions (e.g., managers, directors, and vice presidents) in different fields and industries. They reported a household income higher than $80,000; had seven or more years in the workforce; and 49 percent had an MBA degree. Men and women were equally represented in the assessment tool. We also carried out individual interviews followed by in-depth coaching sessions to validate behavioral attitudes and competencies.

Key findings

Our study revealed the following about emerging Latino leaders' preferred leadership styles: 10 percent showed preference for a more cautious style; 18 percent preferred a competitive style; 24 percent chose a more sociable manner; and 45 percent, the vast majority, were oriented toward a more caring approach. Many displayed a combination of more than one style.

The 10 percent who displayed a cautious leadership style were mostly foreign born, first and some second generation. They remain attached to their country of origin and its traditions but considered themselves bicultural and fully bilingual. Generally introverted and conservative by nature, they favored observation rather than participation. Their mantra was thinking before acting, *El que mucho habla, mucho yerra,* "Who much speaks, much errs." Moreover, they were humble, sincere, and sensitive to those whom they support and lead. These cautious leaders command respect because of who they are rather than what they've accomplished. They preferred slow, formal, structured, and systematic approaches that lead to accuracy.

Of the 18 percent who preferred and exhibited a more competitive leadership style, most were second, third, or later generation Latinos. They viewed themselves as American and were well educated, mostly English dominant with basic Spanish, and assimilated into the mainstream culture. Optimistic, determined, and focused on delivering results, they were often *directo y sincero,* or "straightforward and sincere;" *A Dios rogando y con el mazo dando,* "Praying to God and hitting with the hammer." They were covering all the bases and doing everything necessary to ensure success. Although they showed high levels of competence and professional know-how, they acknowledge having difficulties asking for help. Competitive Latino leaders preferred fast-paced work environments in which they could stay active, grow, and continually learn.

The 24 percent of Latinos who preferred a sociable leadership style were among the most acculturated second and third generation. They tended to have basic Spanish-speaking skills. Resourceful, flexible, and creative, they see themselves as bringing ideas, inspiration, and possibilities *Querer es poder,* "To want to is to be able to." If you really want to do something, you will be able to do it. Enthusiastic team players, their strengths lie in persuasion rather than competition. While they tended to be fashionable and fun to be around, boredom and routine were their nemesis. Sociable Latino leaders seek recognition, flexibility, and interaction.

Latinos who demonstrated the caring leadership style comprised 45 percent of the sample, evenly distributed between men and women. Most were first generation. They displayed strong spiritual and moral foundations and tended to be relaxed, open, patient, and approachable. Hard work, trustworthiness, and integrity were their trademarks. *Buena gente,* or "salt-of-the-earth folks;" *No hay atajo sin trabajo,* "There is no shortcut without work." They valued keeping their word even if it entailed sacrifice. Caring leaders focused on values, fairness, equality, and impartiality in order to maintain harmonious relationships.

Summary

Latino leaders place greater emphasis on family and community than on the individual. Latino leaders have a strong work ethic because they want to provide for and protect their families. They view their responsibilities as a badge of honor and proactively seek opportunities to contribute in a respectful and honorable way at home, at work, and in the community. Latino leaders also value spirituality, compassion, caring, and respect. This approach is comparable with the new leadership paradigms taught by Stephen R. Covey, who writes that the leader of the future is one who creates a culture or value system based on the principles of service, integrity, fairness, and equity. Similarly, Daniel Goleman argues that the most effective leaders are those that possess emotional intelligence—of which empathy and cross-cultural sensitivity are key components.

In the not-too-distant future, Latinos will provide role models in leadership that will complement and challenge perceptions and practices on Main Street and in corporate America. It is yet to be known if future generations will hold on to the Latino heritage, culture, and identities.

Organizations that understand and support Latinos leaders are more likely to retain, develop, and advance them. The results of the study cited above and others like it should have wide impact on the valuation, development, and advancement of Latino leaders. Other studies must be conducted to continue learning about and expanding our understanding of how we can appreciate, value, and better-utilize emerging Latino leaders and what they bring to organizations. However, it is important to understand these issues through the Latino leader's eyes.

CHAPTER 4
A Narrow Pipeline for Latinos

THIS chapter focuses on three key areas: We begin with an overview of the Latino occupational status and earnings gaps. We then examine the narrow pipeline that exists in most organizations today because of the economy or reorganization in favor of a flatter, more competitive, and leaner structure. We conclude by sharing best practices gleaned from companies that are currently adopting development programs to advance Latino leaders.

The weekly earnings report of wages and salaries from the Bureau of Labor Statistics for the first quarter of 2010 shows that among the major racial and ethnic groups, median earnings for Black men working at full time jobs were $635 per week, 73 percent of the median for White men ($869). The difference was slightly less among women, as Black women's median earnings ($584) were 86.1 percent of those for white women ($678). Overall, median earnings of Hispanics who worked full time ($554) were lower than those of Blacks ($610), Whites ($772), and Asians ($859). Research by the Pew Hispanic Center helps to explain the gap between Latinos and other groups:

+ Latino workers are concentrated in nonprofessional service occupations such as building or grounds cleaning and maintenance and food service.

+ Occupations in which Latino workers are concentrated rank low in earnings, educational requirements, and a general measure of socioeconomic status.

+ The occupational status of Mexicans and Puerto Ricans lags the furthest in comparison with the status of Whites. However, Cubans and Whites are comparable in occupational status.

Making the leap from low-paying jobs

A measure of occupational dissimilarity reveals an increasing degree of separation between Latinos and Whites from 1990 to 2000. Whites increased their representation in professional occupations while Latinos trended toward construction and service occupations. Changes in the structure of industries, such as the rise of the technology sectors and the decline of construction and manufacturing, diminished the prospects for upward occupational mobility for Latinos in the 1990s. These shifts also led to a decline for Latinos in employment in several professional occupations with high socioeconomic status such as accounting and engineering.

Education contributes to the improvement of a worker's occupational status, but this is less true for foreign-born Latinos who are faced with challenges such as new immigration policies, new requirements to obtain occupational licenses, lack of technical English capability in their fields, and the need to validate their education completed overseas. It forces recently arrived Latino immigrants to have lower occupational status than previous immigrant waves, even if they have the same educational level and experience. Despite their steady growth in the U.S. population, Latinos are the most underrepresented in the civilian federal employment sector. Latinos account for 8 percent of the total federal workforce even though they now comprise about 15 percent of the U.S. population. Of the 25 largest government agencies, 17 saw modest increases in Latino hires in 2008 over 2007; most of these were made at lower- and mid-level positions. Latinos accounted for 3.6 percent of the Senior Executive Service during 2008, according to the Office of Personnel Management (OPM).

Latinos made progress despite the current economic crisis and the narrow pipeline that exists in corporate America. The U.S. Bureau of Labor Statistics reported that Latinos held 8.1 percent of all management, business, and financial related occupations in 2008, up from 7.7 percent in 2007. Having said this, Latinos have a long way to go in the higher ranks of corporate America. According to the Alliance for Board Diversity (ADB), of the 1,030 people who sat on Fortune 100 boards of directors in 2006, there were only 31 Latinos and 9 Latinas. They represented an increase of 3 people when compared with the 2004 report.

For more than two decades, the Hispanic Association on Corporate Responsibility has advocated for Hispanic inclusion on the boards of directors of the largest 1,000 companies in the United States. It reported that as of December 2009, 78 Hispanics sat on the boards of Fortune 500 companies, accounting for a total of 111 seats, as some held more than one directorship. A total of 20 are Latinas. That means Hispanics hold less than 2 percent of the 5,500 Fortune 500 board seats, despite comprising 15 percent of the nation's population. Among the companies spotlighted by HACR, only nine—AMR Corp., Black & Decker, Edison International, KeyCorp, Manpower, Pitney Bowes, Target, and Winn-Dixie—had more than one Latino director.

The top 40 companies for Latinos

Now let's analyze what some of the top companies for Latinos are doing to develop, train, and advance them in their organizations. Unlike other "Best Company" lists that focus on entry-level hiring, *Latino Business Magazine's* top 40 companies list is based on an in-depth analysis of 30 critical statistics that measure a company's commitment to Latinos in the workplace and examines how companies reach Latinos in recruitment, promotion, retention, procurement, community support, and consumer marketing.

These companies have several elements in common, including accessible career development programs and fast-track trainee programs to provide upward mobility within the company. They also have a strong Latino presence at the highest levels of the company's management. Many have visible role models at the top that actively mentor Latino talent. Equally as important, many offer certain flexibilities and benefits that aid in the retention of qualified Latinos, such as part-time employment or lateral moves from one area to another within the same company for personal or professional development reasons. Many offer extended family and domestic partner benefits.

For instance, McDonald's Corporation has over 22,000 women, including Latinas, working for the company at all levels of employment, including the boardroom and executive offices. Women are recruited through targeted ads that run in both English and Spanish at the local and national level. McDonald's Corporation also has a college internship program that recruits potential operations leaders. The company provides mentoring and leadership training through its Hispanic Mentoring Program, Hispanic Leadership Council, and resource groups, as well as the Women's Career Development Class. Additionally, the company's Accelerated Operations Program seeks to identify a diverse group of high-performing employees to serve as future leaders for McDonald's restaurant operations. Latinas employed at the company can take advantage of the continuous education reimbursements that the company provides to its employees.

Bank of America is another company doing a stellar job developing and advancing Latinos. Senior executive management ties incentive pay to progress in hiring, promoting, and retaining diverse individuals. Women, people of color, gay/lesbian/bisexual/transgender associates, disabled persons, and veterans serve at the highest levels of the company's management. The bank focuses its efforts on diversity and inclusion through regional councils, more than 50 diversity networks, and nine affinity groups that support each member's development and success. The bank offers extended family and domestic partner benefits and has an equal opportunity policy that includes a nondiscrimination clause based on sexual orientation and gender identity. It collaborates with national multicultural professional associations, such as the National Association of Hispanic MBAs, to recruit talent and develop business relationships. Businesses owned by minorities, women, veterans, and disabled persons are given the opportunity to participate in the procurement activities of Bank of America.

Figure 4.1 The Top 40 Best Companies for Latino Employment

McDonald's Corporation	Prudential Financial
Bank of America	United Parcel Service, Inc.
SBC Communications Inc.	PacifiCare Health Systems
Washington Mutual, Inc.	Comcast Corporation
Verizon Communications	Consolidated Edison, Inc.
Sodexo, Inc.	Xerox
Wells Fargo	American Express Company
Darden Restaurants	Kellogg Company
Citigroup, Inc.	Tribune Company
Marriott International, Inc.	IBM Corp.
Denny's Restaurants	Coors Brewing Company
Global Hyatt Corporation	Affiliated Computer Services, Inc.
PG&E Corporation	HSBC North America Holdings, Inc.
The Coca-Cola Company	Aramark
Bellsouth Corporation	Lucent Technologies
PepsiCo	Intel Corporation
Freddie Mac	Tech Data Corp
MGM Mirage	Bausch & Lomb
Allstate Insurance Company	Teachers Insurance and Annuity Assoc.
General Mills	American Electric Power

Source: Latino Business Magazine

Summary

President Obama is appointing more Latinos in his administration than any president in American history. This serves as a testament to the demographic changes taking place in the marketplace However, it may take 70 to 100 years to achieve parity with other groups. This narrow pipeline exists for Latinos in most organizations today because of the slow economic growth, reorganization in favor of a flatter, more competitive, and leaner structure.

The length of time that foreign-born Latinos have been in the U.S. contributes to a narrowing of the gap in occupational status with respect to Whites.

Assimilation into the business world proves to be fastest for those who are more educated, whereas those who are less educated rarely fully assimilate into a corporate culture. Second and third generation Latinos have greater access to higher education and scholarships. It is fair to expect the next generation of Latinos to be more educated, but they will have to prove themselves in line positions and in high-profile jobs and assignments to make the leap from low-paying jobs to higher executive levels.

We conclude by sharing best practices gleaned from companies that are currently adopting development programs to advance Latino leaders.

+ Discover where you stand. Determine how many Latinos you have in managerial jobs and how many you have in senior leadership positions. Does your leadership look like your customer base? If not, you may be missing significant opportunities.

+ Check your pipeline. Look at your talent pipeline to see if you are recruiting, retaining, and advancing enough emerging Latinos leaders to move your company into the future.

+ Make a leadership commitment. Let everyone in your organization know that senior management is committed to diversity with official statements, policies, programs and, most important, actions. Hold leaders accountable for results, not just intentions.

+ Support mentoring. Partner senior executives with Latinos through internal mentoring programs or outside programs.

+ Give middle managers the training, support, and motivation they need to advance emerging Latino leaders. Enlist them in the planning of diversity initiatives, and reinforce the fact that diversity impacts everyone's bottom line.

+ Create educational programs for Latino leaders to serve, train, and network within your organization and throughout the industry.

+ Ensure Latino leaders have a seat at the decision-making table as individuals, and recognize their combined wisdom through affinity networks and events.

- Determine actionable ways to help improve the visibility of Latino managers in your organization and industry.

- Partner with advocacy groups, sponsor scholarships, adopt a school, donate products, support charities, and become an active partner in the communities where your employees and customers live. Highlight best practices for your organization with these groups.

CHAPTER 5

Breaking the Glass Ceiling

LATINOS have made a lot of progress thanks to the Women's Rights movement, the Civil Rights movements, the Glass Ceiling Act, the Lilly Ledbetter Fair Pay Restoration Act, and the support of many men and women in positions of power who embraced multiculturalism and the belief that America is founded by immigrants. However, discrimination based on race, ethnicity, gender, and sexual orientation continues to be part of the fabric of American life. While many have welcomed the change and embraced Latin music, food, and traditions, the growth of the Latino population in the last ten years has resulted in many other Americans feeling threatened by how Latinos have changed American culture and identity, and blame them for lowering wages.

The purpose of the Glass Ceiling Commission was to determine whether a glass ceiling existed and, if it did, to identify the barriers to placing more women and minorities in senior management positions. The same barriers it identified exist in the work environment today when it comes to advancing women and minorities to senior levels. They include social barriers, limited access to educational opportunities, and biases related to gender, race, and ethnicity. There are also organizational barriers such as internal structural shortcomings in the execution of corporate practices of hiring, developing, and advancing women and minorities.

The organizational culture and internal politics may exclude women and minorities from activities that will lead to advancement, such as mentoring and coaching, management training, or career development assignments. The last barrier is governmental—inconsistent enforcement of equal opportunity legislation and poor collection and dissemination of statistics.

To overcome these barriers, companies require the full support of their CEOs and senior management, the integration of diversity as part of the strategic planning of the organization, and holding management accountable for achieving goals by tracking and reporting on progress. Even though top leaders, CEOs, and presidents understand and support the act, it has never been given so much attention until now, the Obama era.

Presidential Proclamation: National Equal Pay Day, April 20, 2010

Throughout our Nation's history, extraordinary women have broken barriers to achieve their dreams and blazed trails so their daughters would not face similar obstacles. . . . Despite decades of progress, pay inequity still hinder women and their families across our country. . . . Our Nation's workforce includes more women than ever before. In households across the country, many women are the sole breadwinner, or share this role equally with their partner. However, wage discrimination still exists. Nearly half of all working Americans are women, yet they earn only about 80 cents for every dollar men earn. This gap increases among minority women and those with disabilities.

Pay inequity is not just an issue for women; American families, communities, and our entire economy suffer as a result of this disparity. We are still recovering from our economic crisis, and many hardworking Americans are still feeling its effects. Too many families are struggling to pay their bills or put food on the table, and this challenge should not be exacerbated by discrimination. I was proud that the first bill I signed into law, the Lilly Ledbetter Fair Pay Restoration Act in 2009, helps women achieve wage fairness. This law brings us closer to ending pay disparities based on gender, age, race, ethnicity, religion, or disability by allowing more individuals to challenge inequality.

NOW, THEREFORE, I, BARACK OBAMA, President of the United States of America, by virtue of the authority vested in me by the Constitution and the laws of the United States, do hereby proclaim April 20, 2010, as National Equal Pay Day. I call upon all Americans to

acknowledge the injustice of wage discrimination and join my Administration's efforts to achieve equal pay for equal work.

Latinos breaking the glass ceiling

Senator Robert Dole introduced legislation known as the Glass Ceiling Act
that was signed into law as an amendment to Title II of the Civil Rights Act
of 1991. But in 1981 the very first Latinos had already broken the glass ceiling in corporate America. Cuban-born Roberto Goizueta was appointed CEO
of Coca-Cola. He was born on November 18, 1931, in Havana to Crispulo
Goizueta and Aida Cantera. His father owned a sugar plantation and was
wealthy enough to send him to a small preparatory school in New Hampshire.
There young Goizueta learned to speak English partly by watching movies.
After he graduated as class valedictorian, he attended Yale University in New
Haven, Connecticut, to study chemical engineering. He received his bachelor
of science degree in 1953, shortly before marrying Olga Casteleiro. The couple
eventually had three children. Goizueta returned to Cuba in 1954, but instead
of working on his family's sugar plantation, he became the technical director
of the Coca-Cola plant in Havana. The Goizueta family's circumstances were
soon changed by a social revolution that swept across Cuba.

   In 1960, Goizueta fled to Miami, Florida where he worked as an engineer
for Coke's Latin American operations. Goizueta was promoted to the Atlanta
world headquarters in 1964, where he became well known in management
ranks for having a tidy desk at the end of every business day and wearing
well-tailored suits. In 1979, he was promoted to vice president, and became
responsible for several different areas of the company, including its laboratories
and legal department. Over the next fifteen years, Goizueta steadily climbed
the corporate ladder. By 1980, he had become Coca-Cola's president and chief
operating officer (COO). He became chief executive officer (CEO) in 1981, a
move that surprised many in the business world, in part because he was the
first head of Coca-Cola who did not come from its Georgia headquarters.

In addition, corporate analysts questioned the move since many of his leadership duties would involve marketing, an area in which Goizueta had virtually no experience. Yet because of time spent heading the Coca-Cola labs, he did possess one advantage over his fellow contenders: he was familiar with what was called "the knowledge" in company lore—Coca-Cola's highly secretive formula. Reportedly he was one of only two people in the company who knew it.

In the end, Goizueta did prove to be a savvy marketing executive. When he took the reins, Coca-Cola was losing market share to its major competitor, Pepsi, and its stock was not performing well. Although it had a strong international presence, Coke's brand image was perceived as old-fashioned and conservative. Goizueta reversed all of these problems.

One of his first decisions was to allow a new diet drink to trade on the success of the Coke name, and so Diet Coke was introduced in 1982. Goizueta also launched aggressive marketing campaigns that helped to reverse Pepsi's gains in market share and Coke sales tripled. Finally, he focused on stock performance and succeeded in keeping Coca-Cola shareholders happy with a healthy annual return on their investment. From 1981 to 1997 the company's stock value increased over 7,000 percent.

Source: www.referenceforbusiness.com

CEO material

Why aren't there more Latinos at the top? The reality is that the odds of making it to the top are always slim, regardless of one's background. Certainly, it is not the lack of talented individuals; rather, the answer has more to do with business strategies and learning how to position, develop, and advance Latino leaders. Latinos are not making it to the top fast enough because of the challenges they have to overcome, including managing corporate politics, obtaining visible positions, and finding role models.

An article written by Jeff Zbar in March 2010 in Poder360° headlined, "Cracking the C-Suite, Reaching the top echelons of fortune 1000 companies is proving a challenge for Hispanics" noted that Hispanic represent only about 1 percent of the CEOs among the biggest U.S. corporations. How did these Latino leaders make it through the narrow pipeline? The answer may be twofold: formal education and the burning desire to succeed.

These CEOs spent the early stages of their careers learning the intricacies of the corporate world by themselves, not from their parents. They took educated and visible risks; they were accountable for their performance; and they made contributions that could be objectively measured, such as production quotas, sales revenue, product launches, and on-time delivery. And they had long tenure with the company or industry in which they became named CEOs.

Success is possible regardless of being foreign born or native born. Here is a list of the top 15 Latino executives currently employed in corporate America, highlights of their contributions and educational background.

Antonio M. Perez
Chairman, President, and CEO, Eastman Kodak

Mr. Perez has presided over Eastman Kodak at a time when its very existence was in jeopardy. Where once the company's film-based business could have been its downfall, today Kodak reportedly is the leading seller of digital cameras in the U.S. and third in the world. At Kodak he has moved strongly into consumer inkjet printers, sensors for digital cameras and mobile phones, and solutions for retail, commercial and workflow applications—generating 2008 revenues of $6 billion. A Spanish native, Perez studied marketing, business and electronic engineering in both Spain and France.

Source: www.poder360.com

Cristóbal I. Conde
President and CEO, SunGard Data Systems

Mr Cristóbal I. Conde is a progressive thinker in the corporate workplace. A believer in a flattened, collaborative environment, he empowers his people and uses technology, but encourages open discourse, free thinking, and the well-written document. Conde arrived at SunGard in 1987 after the company acquired Devon Systems International Inc., whose technology solutions served the interest rate and currency derivatives markets. Beyond SunGard, Conde is a member of the Clinton Global Initiative. Conde was born in Chile, is a U.S. citizen, and earned his B.S. degree in Astronomy and Physics from Yale University.

Source: www.poder360.com

Manuel Medina-Mora
CEO, Citi Consumer Banking for the Americas

He took over Citi's core consumer banking business in January 2010. He is also responsible for working with regional directors globally to oversee Citi's consumer strategy worldwide. Medina-Mora, a native of Mexico, previously led the company's banking operations in Latin America, where he earned the trust of Vikram Pandit, the company's top executive. In the U.S., Medina-Mora will take over 1,000 branches serving American and Canadian consumers, with over $139 billion in deposits and $34 billion under management.

Source: www.poder360.com

Ralph de la Vega
President and CEO, AT&T Mobility & Consumer Markets

He has made his career in technology and telecommunications. It was as the COO of the former Cingular Wireless that de la Vega oversaw the merger between the company and AT&T. With that success, he was named in 2004 Executive of the Year by the Association of Latino Professionals in Finance and Accounting. The Cuban native earned his degree in mechanical engineering from Florida Atlantic University after fleeing the island to Miami as a child without his parents or siblings.

Source: www.poder360.com

Paul J. Díaz,
President and CEO, Kindred Healthcare, Inc.

An attorney and accountant, Paul J. Díaz oversees one of the country's largest providers of long-term healthcare services. Previously he held a variety of executive posts, including Executive vice president/ COO with Mariner Health, and president of its Inpatient Division. Before Mariner Health, he was CEO, CFO, and General Counsel of Allegis Health Services. Diaz is a graduate of the Kogod College of Business Administration at American University and received his Law degree from Georgetown University.

Source: www.poder360.com

Fernando Aguirre
Chairman and CEO, Chiquita Brands International, Inc.

He became CEO in January 2004. He is responsible for setting the company's day-to-day operational performance and its strategic direction. Prior to Chiquita, Mr. Aguirre spent more than 23 years in brand and general management and turnarounds at Procter & Gamble (P&G). He began with P&G in Mexico in 1980, rising through the corporation in positions which included the leader of P&G's first Hispanic Marketing Group, president and GM of P&G Brazil, Vice-President of P&G's global and U.S. snacks and food products, and president of global feminine care. In July 2002, Fernando Aguirre was named president of special projects, reporting directly to P&G's Chairman and CEO. A native of Mexico, Aguirre earned his Bachelor of Science degree in business administration and marketing from Southern Illinois University.

Source: www.siue.edu/alumni/aboutalumni/aguirrefernando.shtml

Richard L. Carrión,
Chairman and CEO, Popular, Inc.

He became Chief Executive Officer (1989) and Chairman (1993) of Popular Inc. and Banco Popular de Puerto Rico; member of the Board of Directors of Verizon; Director of the Federal Reserve Bank of New York; Chairman of the Board of Banco Popular Foundation. He has a B.S. in Economics, Wharton School of Finance and Commerce, University of Pennsylvania and an M.S. in Management Information Systems, Massachusetts Institute of Technology.

Source: http://people.forbes.com/profile/richard-l-carrion/64615

Linda A. Lang
Chairman and CEO, Jack in the Box, Inc.

The only Latina to make the list, she is chairman of the board and chief executive officer of Jack in the Box, Inc., a restaurant company that operates and franchises Jack in the Box restaurants, one of the nation's largest hamburger chains. Since joining Jack in the Box in 1984, Ms. Lang has held various positions of increasing responsibility in marketing, operations and finance. Previously president and chief operating officer, she was named chairman and CEO in October 2005. In 2008, Ms. Lang was recognized by *Forbes.com* as one of the top 10 female CEOs in the country. She was also recognized by *Latino Leaders* magazine in 2008 as one of the top candidates for service on corporate boards and she was recognized by *Hispanic Business* magazine as one of its 2008 Women of the Year. In 2007, *Nation's Restaurant News* honored Ms. Lang with a Golden Chain Award for her achievements and career accomplishments. Ms. Lang has a master's degree in business administration from San Diego State University and a bachelor's degree in finance from the University of California, Berkeley.

Source: www.calstate.edu/BOT/bios/lang.shtml

Gerardo I. (Gerry) Lopez
CEO and Director, AMC Entertainment Holdings, Inc.

He has served as Chief Executive Officer and President of AMC Entertainment Holdings since March 2009, when he was also elected to the company's Board of Directors. Lopez is only the fourth CEO in the company's almost 90-year history. Prior to joining AMC, Lopez served as executive vice president of Starbucks Coffee Company and president of its Global Consumer Products, Seattle's Best Coffee and Foodservice divisions. Lopez's management philosophy is simple: hire good people, agree on a direction, provide the tools, and reward results. His mantra, as he puts it, is to "listen, learn, discuss, decide, execute, measure and . . . repeat." Lopez has been recognized by *Hispanic Business Magazine* as one of the Top 100 Hispanic Business Leaders. A native of Oriente, Cuba, and a current resident of Kansas City, Missouri, Lopez earned his B.S. in business administration from George Washington University and his MBA from Harvard Business School.

Source: www.investor.amctheatres.com/management.cfm

Antonio Lucio
Chief Marketing Officer, VISA Inc.

Antonio Lucio directs all branding and marketing activities for Visa Inc. Lucio has more than 25 years of global marketing and brand management experience, earned at some of the world's most successful consumer packaged goods companies including PepsiCo, Kraft, General Foods, RJR Foods International, and Procter & Gamble. Most recently he was chief innovation and health and wellness officer for PepsiCo. Lucio earned a B.A. in history from Louisiana State University in 1981. He was born in Spain, raised in Puerto Rico, and educated in the United States. Lucio is fluent in English, Spanish, and Portuguese.

Source: http://corporate.visa.com/about-visa/executive-leadership/antonio-lucio.shtml

J. Mario Molina
Chairman, President, and CEO, Molina Healthcare, Inc.

Joseph M. Molina, MD, is President and Chief Executive Officer of Molina Healthcare, Inc. In 1980, his father, C. David Molina, MD, founded Molina Healthcare to address the special needs of low-income patients. After his father's death in 1996, Dr. Molina was elected Chairman of the Board and assumed the chief executive role at Molina Healthcare. In 2002, Dr. Molina was inducted into the Long Beach Community College Hall of Fame. In 2005 he was featured in *Time* magazine as one of the 25 most influential Hispanics in America. Dr. Molina received his degree from the University of Southern California and performed his internship and residency at Johns Hopkins Hospital in Maryland.

Source: www.molinahealthcare.com/abtmolina/who/lead/pages/jmario.aspx

Manuel J. Perez de la Mesa
President and CEO, Pool Corporation

Mr. Perez de la Mesa, a Cuban immigrant, has been Chief Executive Officer since May 2001 and has also been President since February 1999. Previously, he had general, financial and operations management experience with Watsco, Inc. from 1994 to 1999, Fresh Del Monte Produce B.V. from 1987 to 1994, International Business Machines Corp. from 1982 to 1987, and Sea-Land

Service Inc./R.J. Reynolds Industries, Inc. from 1977 to 1982. He has a Bachelor of Business Administration, Florida International University and a Masters of Business Administration, St. John's University.

Source: http://people.forbes.com/profile/manuel-j-perez-de-la-mesa/64595

Josue (Joe) Robles, Jr.
President and CEO, United Services Automobile Association

"Joe" Robles is president and chief executive officer of USAA, one of America's leading financial services companies. He was named CFO and controller in September 1994, and added corporate treasurer to his responsibilities in 1995. He assumed the position of president and CEO in December 2007. Born in Rio Piedras, Puerto Rico, Robles joined the U.S. Army in 1966. For the next 28 years, he served in a variety of command and staff positions, including active duty posts in Korea, Vietnam, Germany, and Operations Desert Shield and Desert Storm in the Middle East. In 2009, *The Christian Science Monitor* named Robles the "No. 1 Veteran in Business" and *American Banker* named him "Innovator of the Year." Robles serves on several non profit boards. Robles holds a bachelor of business administration degree in accounting from Kent State University and a master's degree in business administration from Indiana State University.

Source: www.fastcompany.com/mba/node/18.

Gabriel Tirador
President, CEO, and Director, Mercury General Corporation

Mr. Tirador has been President since October 2001 and its Chief Executive Officer since January 2007. Mr. Tirador serves as Chief Financial Officer of Mercury Insurance Company. Mr. Tirador served as Chief Operating Officer of Mercury General Corp. since October 2001. Mr. Tirador served as Mercury General Corp.'s assistant Controller from March 1994 to December 1996. He served as the Vice President and Controller of the Automobile Club of Southern California. Mr. Tirador is a Certified Public Accountant.

Source: http://investing.businessweek.com/businessweek

Alberto J. Verme
CEO, Citi Europe, Middle East, and Africa

Verme's focus is on Central and Eastern Europe and the 21 countries in the Middle East region. He is responsible for the performance of all of Citi's businesses in EMEA. He is a member of Citi's Senior Leadership Committee. A Peruvian national, Verme received a BA in Economics from Denison University in 1979 and an MBA from Columbia Business School in 1984. He began his career at The World Bank in 1979. He is a member of the Citi Foundation Board of Directors, Columbia Business School London Advisory Board, and Columbia Business School Board of Overseers in the United States.

Source: www.citigroup.com/citi/corporategovernance/profiles/verme/index.htm

Career killers

Julio Ortiz works at a pharmaceutical company. He relocated from Mexico to work at its headquarters in the United States. An extremely well educated and successful man, Julio experienced culture shock when he came to work in America. He could not understand the whole concept of performance achievement. In Mexico, he had worked just as hard but with less stress and competition. His job is all consuming, leaving no time for family. In Mexico, he had felt he was part of a group that helped each other, but here, he felt disposable.

Julio's story is not unique. Both native-born and non-native individuals have to learn to navigate American corporate culture. They may experience performance gaps if they are not assigned a mentor, don't have the benefit of a company's resource group, or don't join professional associations.

Reliable statistics are not available regarding Latino professionals facing the glass ceiling within their organizations. Although the number of Latinos in senior management positions has improved over the last 10 years, the total number is not encouraging. Among the professional corporate clientele we surveyed for this book, the most common career killers were the invisibility syndrome, stereotypes, and forced assimilation.

The invisibility syndrome results from the lack of role models, mentors, and networking opportunities. Latinos were passed over for key assignments and promotions because they did not have high-profile role models and Latino mentors to help pave the way. Many resented when Latino talent was brought in from the outside, thinking that the organization did not do enough to develop its own Latino talent pool. Creating effective and efficient networks and affinity groups would mitigate the invisibility syndrome.

The stereotype that Latinos are hard workers but not leaders prevents them from accessing leadership roles in important projects and assignments in which they can prove themselves, and in which they can connect to informal networks—both important stepping-stones to higher corporate positions.

Bosses and peers sometimes deliver the direct or indirect message that Latinos must blend in order to get ahead. Asking Latinos to downplay an identifiable accent in the corporate environment is a kind of forced assimilation. Micro-inequities is a term that's being used for small but hurtful discrimination and forcing people to lose their accent is a good example.

Silvia Rodriguez's experience exemplifies this. Sylvia transferred from Mexico City, Mexico to the North American headquarters of a consumer products company. Her boss hired her because he liked her knowledge of the Latin American marketplace, her MBA in marketing, and her native Spanish. During her very first presentation, some of her peers made fun of her accent, repeating the words she mispronounced. Her accent was perceived as an indication of limited intelligence or capability that had an impact on her contributions. As a result, she retreated and isolated herself for two years.

Current negative attitudes toward undocumented immigration in the United States may create a particularly unfavorable atmosphere for speakers with Latino accents (Davila et al., 1993), regardless of citizenship status. People are quick to appraise someone's intelligence by their appearance. This includes not only the way they look, but also the way they communicate, and how truthful the message is perceived. Accent might reduce the credibility of non-native job seekers, eyewitnesses, actors, reporters, and news anchors.

In the United States, Title VII of the Civil Rights Act of 1964 prohibits discrimination based on national origin, but it does not specifically mention accents (Matsuda, 1991; Nguyen, 1993). For instance, Wated and Sanchez (2006) found that possessing a non-native accent served as a significant predictor of stress experienced at work for Hispanic workers in the United States.

From the often-abrasive judge on *American Idol* whose criticisms seem somehow more palatable because of his flawless delivery to Geico's commercials that feature a gecko with a refined accent who sells car insurance, it's clear that American culture is obsessed with accents. A refined English accent and superior vocabulary is considered synonymous with a higher IQ, but is this the case? Perhaps it is the opposite. People from other cultures that read, write, and comprehend more than one language are more cross-culturally proficient. Foreign-born individuals like California Governor Arnold Schwarzenegger overcame his accent and secured the trust of voters. Antonio Bandera won the Oscar in 2005 and Penelope Cruz won in 2009; Cristina Vergara in her supporting role in the comedy, *Modern Family*, has been nominated for several awards, just to name a few who have overcome this negative stigma.

In July, 2010 the University of Chicago released a report about research published in the *Journal of Experimental Social Psychology* by Shiri Lev-Ari and Boaz Keysar. The researchers found in a small study that people unconsciously doubt statements in accents that they find difficult to understand more than ones delivered in accents that are completely familiar. "Instead of perceiving the statements as more difficult to understand, they perceive them as less truthful," the researchers said. These results have important implications for how people perceive non-native speakers of a language, particularly as mobility increases in the modern world, leading millions of people to be non-native speakers of the language they use daily.

Commenting on the study in an interview in the *Montreal Gazette*, Agata Gluszek, a PhD candidate at Yale University, said that accents from Asian countries and Central and South American are generally perceived more negatively in both the United States and Canada. "It's not to say there isn't discrimination against ethnicity and race, it's just not acceptable socially (like accent discrimination)," she said.

On one hand, those whose accents are less well understood may experience more problems in communicating and therefore have less successful interactions, or avoid them completely. On the other hand, understanding may play only a limited role and subjective comprehensibility may have more influence on the interaction (Rubin, 1992).

English is and will continue to be the international language of business. However, we are a multilingual country, and we need to get used to hearing more than one accent at the office without biases or prejudice. Conversely, some jobs require that employees speak Spanish with international partners, customers, and suppliers. Bilingual employees are a valuable asset to organizations that do business with Spanish-speaking associates. Many bilingual Latinos are not encouraged or compensated for bringing this additional talent as the translator or interpreter for many managers and organizations.

A respondent to our research, *The Emerging Latino Leader: Attitudes and Behaviors in the Workplace*, often went above and beyond his job description in this capacity. Yet, he was neither recognized nor compensated for this contribution. He suggested providing additional step payment for speaking a second language or being bilingual, and an additional payment when bilingual employees provide language services for the organization, which would demonstrate measurable appreciation of this skill. Certainly, any organization that deliberately hires bilingual employees should not discourage them from speaking Spanish in the workplace.

Inter-Latino group dynamics

Currently, there are Latinos from many countries in the United States and they are neither a homogeneous group, nor do they all like each other. Prejudice among inter-Latino groups is a complex issue and may be confusing to non-Latinos who cluster Latinos into one group. Colonialism, socioeconomic differences, educational levels, political issues, and regional labels all contribute to inter-Latino prejudice. It can be challenging for an organization to identify inter-Latino tension or prejudice in a business setting. To do so requires human resource experts, diversity and inclusion departments, and the understanding of management to discern if there are nuances among Mexicans, Puerto Ricans, Cubans, and Dominicans, just to name a few.

A good way to help understand the different Latinos identities comes from a model created by Fedman and Gallegos in 2007 titled "Identity Orientations of Latinos in the United States, Implications for Leaders and Organizations," in *The Business Journal of Hispanic Research*. The researchers described six groups, summarized briefly as follows:

+ **Undifferentiated orientation:** Tend to see themselves as "just people" or "color blind" and accept the dominant social norms without challenging them or deny cultural differences.

+ **White-identified:** May be assimilated completely into the white culture and sometimes disconnect themselves from other Latinos. May be connected to a particular Latino subgroup; they feel superior to other ethnic or racial groups.

+ **Latino as "other":** Individuals that according to the research "may not be familiar with or adhere closely to the Latino culture or values, but do not feel connected to White cultural values either"; they may identify with people of color in more generic terms.

+ **"Sub-group" orientation:** See themselves primarily in terms of their ethnic group or nationality, for example, Mexican or Cuban or Puerto Rican. May see other sub-groups as inferior. Nationality, ethnicity, and culture play a large role. This group sees Whites as barriers to full inclusion or as unimportant to their day-to-day jobs.

+ **Latino-identified orientation:** Tend to see Latinos as a distinct racial category across all Latino sub groups; as a result they see the similarities and connections in a broad sense that transcends cultural differences, making them open to other points of view. They may see whites as allies or barriers depending on key behaviors. This group tends to be a strong advocate for Latino issues.

+ **Latino-integrated orientation:** Deals very well with the complexity of their Latino identity and rich culture. Their perception is that they are fully integrated with other social identities such as faith, gender, and social classes. Moreover they understand and relate well with other cultures and recognize that Latino is just one of many identities. They are also careful not to impose their way of being to others. In that respect they make clear choices on how to interact in any given situation, sometimes comfortably acting out of their Latino identity. It appears that they see culture identity as one part of their status as multidimensional leaders.

Navigating corporate politics

Establishing political connections, informal networks, and coalitions are not familiar activities for Latinos. They value humility, and as a result, playing politics and self-promotion does not come naturally to them. Traditional Latino beliefs dictate that if they work hard and put their fates in God's hands, then their bosses will reward them accordingly. If Latinos do not learn to think of politics as part of their jobs and assume only performance matters, they will fail. What can your organization do to educate Latinos about navigating corporate politics? The following insights are based on ones we use in our executive coaching program when counseling Latino leaders about how to deal with office politics. Encourage your organization's leadership to employ these concepts to support Latino advancement.

- First, acknowledge its existence; politics comes with the job.
- Encourage your Latino employees to develop their own "Brand" (discussed in Chapter 8). This includes learning how to promote themselves by capitalizing on strengths and contributions and how to communicate those messages to peers and superiors.
- Provide support. A more senior and well-connected mentor can demonstrate the proper way to play politics since each organization is different, and what may be acceptable at one organization may not be acceptable at another. This is especially true if Latino leaders are switching units or jobs or are assigned to new projects.
- Help them face confrontation head on. Friction with a strong personality is inevitable. If it is a new boss, this means understanding what he

or she wants and how to get on board with his or her vision, mission, values, strategies, and critical initiatives as soon as possible.

+ Help them connect up. Latino employees should know the movers and shakers in the organization.

+ Make it clear that connecting down is equally important. Developing strong relationships with others at all levels, from the janitor to the boardroom, is a vital skill.

+ Encourage them to get involved. Senior managers are impressed by staff who cross departmental lines, show initiative, and expand their skill set. Encourage Latino leaders to pursue activities that expand their visibility, credibility, and trustworthiness.

+ Make it clear that networking is critical. Certain social constructs in Latino culture can make networking difficult; this is discussed in further detail in Chapter 7. The absence of this critical competency may hinder Latino leaders' advancement opportunities because they are not perceived as an insider or part of the "Old Boys Club."

+ Model leadership behavior. Know the big picture; understand current challenges, be assertive, honest, and a direct communicator. Make it clear through your behavior that these attributes are desirable and that Latino employees who follow your example will be recognized accordingly.

+ Help them feel comfortable on stage. Public-speaking skills are essential to moving up the corporate ladder. Encourage your employees to join a Toastmasters group to fine-tune their skills.

Summary

Government agencies, businesses, and other organizations have made great progress toward creating a diverse workforce, though many fall short on inclusion strategies. Inclusion strategies such as multicultural leadership training will spawn a new breed of leaders who will value the world views and behaviors of others and learn, accept, adapt, and integrate them into their own views and behaviors. These multicultural leaders will operate with a clear understanding that their thoughts, ideas, and points of view are colored by their cultural biases; accept themselves and others for who they are; show dignity and respect for all; and create productive environments that encourage inclusion and cross-pollination. As a result, multicultural leaders will capture the advantages of a diverse workforce; optimize shareholder value; and promote ethical, social, and environmentally responsible practices.

Organizations need to create an inclusive environment so they can spend less time overcoming stereotypes and more time contributing to the bottom line. Senior management can develop inclusiveness by ensuring multicultural leadership competencies are communicated, resources are provided, and opportunities are equally distributed. Managers at all levels should be trained to address discrimination in every form in the workplace; organizations should not rely solely on their human resources team or their diversity and inclusion department to resolve or prevent potential litigation. Diversity efforts should educate everyone regardless of their race, ethnicity, gender, or sexual orientation. Finally, ensure Latinos have a forum to familiarize themselves with the organization's political culture and help them navigate it.

CHAPTER 6

The Latino Competency Model

OUR passion is to understand the relationship between generations and acculturation and the common behaviors that accompany Latinos in America as they relate to leadership. In particular, we are interested in Latino Millennial and Fusionistas as they become an active part of the workforce and society. Unlike other minority groups, such as African Americans who have internationally renowned leaders like Martin Luther King, Jr., Latinos look to their family members as role models.

Andrés Tapia in his 2009 book, *The Inclusion Paradox*, finds that the "weaknesses in the multicultural talent pipeline also reflect the weakness of overall leadership development. If we don't have strong leadership development programs, it doesn't matter what kind of focus we have on filling the pipeline with diverse talent. Progress will be hampered"

In 2009 we decided to develop a tool we called the Latino Competency Model (LCM) as part of our leadership workshops to help companies value, develop, and advance Latino professionals and retain their employees.

The foundation for this model came from *The Emerging Latino Leader: Attitudes and Behaviors in the Workplace* study mentioned earlier that looked at the unique dynamics of factors influencing Latino leadership behaviors—such as the original archetypes on whom they modeled leadership and the connection among Latino values, behaviors, and leadership capability.

The study revealed that 10 percent showed preferences for a more-cautious, wiser style, 18 percent preferred a competitive, boss-like style, 24 percent chose a more sociable-partnership manner, and 45 percent, the vast majority, were oriented toward a more caring-team or teacher approach. Many displayed a combination of more than one style. The description of the Latino values that are factored into the LCM includes a caveat: There is a great diversity of Latinos in the United States, generations, and different cultures that may express values in different ways.

The Business Journal of Hispanic Research in 2008 published an article entitled, "Self-Observer Rating Discrepancies on the Derailment Behaviors of Hispanic Managers." This research study used self observations to compare the characteristics and behaviors of Hispanic managers whose promotions were derailed to managers from other ethnic groups (Whites, Blacks, and Asians) whose workplace success was derailed. Lombardo and McCauley (1988) indicated that derailment occurs "when a manager who was expected to go higher in the organization and who was judged to have the ability to do so is fired, demoted, or plateaued below expected levels of achievement."

Our two studies, *The Emerging Latino Leader: Attitudes and Behaviors in the Workplace*, and *Latina as Corporate Leader* validated the most frequent reasons for derailments applicable to Latino leaders in general:

- **Problems with interpersonal relationships:** Latinos who isolate themselves from others or who are described as authoritarian, cold, aloof, arrogant, and insensitive.

- **Trouble leading a team:** Latinos who fail to staff effectively, fail to build or to properly lead a team, and are unable to handle conflict.

- **Difficulty changing or adapting:** Latinos who are unable to adapt to a boss with a different managerial or interpersonal style, those who are inflexible or unable to grow, learn, develop, and have difficulty adapting to a more assertive strategic thinking business requirement.

- **Failure to meet business objectives:** Latinos who are overly ambitious, lack follow-through, or are poor performers in general.

- **Narrow functional orientation:** Latinos who are unprepared for promotion and are unable to manage outside of their current function or who do not possess the strategic vision to move their units forward.

The Latino Competency Model is a platform for leadership development, beginning from the inside and moving outward.

At the center are four archetypes: Sabio/Wise; Jefe/Boss; Socio/Partner; and Maestro/Teacher. The first layer outlines the common cultural leadership values that a Latino employee may exhibit in the workplace. Some exhibit them to a higher degree than others depending on their gender, education, generation, socioeconomic level, and country of origin. The second layer refers to global leadership, and each capability is defined by a set of competencies. This model creates a common language for discussion that benefits both the organization and the Latino leader and provides the following benefits:

+ Helps Latino leaders and the organization understand key behaviors, potential derailments, and expectations for roles.

+ Motivates Latino employees to improve specific competencies for professional development.

+ Stimulates Latino employees to use those competencies that are natural to them.

+ Protects morale by quantifying and creating a common understanding of expected performance levels at each career stage.

+ Implements and communicates Latino leadership development strategies.

+ Sets expectations for current Latino leaders and serves as a framework for the development of those in the organization who aspire to become senior leaders.

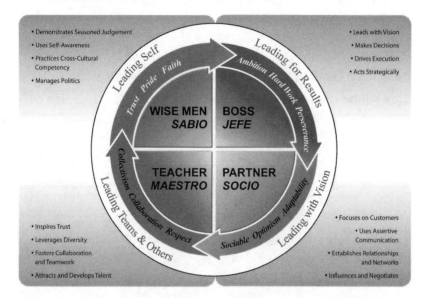

The term "competencies" refers to behaviors and skills beyond technical expertise or know-how that are necessary in a particular role. The Leadership Competency Model, details key competencies and behaviors that are directly influenced by a particular archetype and values. Based on our experience these competencies should sound familiar to most organizations, although they will vary in depth and scope from one organization to another. We clustered the four capabilities with the most critical competencies as follows:

Leading Self

Key competencies: Demonstrates seasoned judgment, uses self-awareness, practices cross-cultural competency and manages politics.

Leading Others and Teams

Key competencies: Inspires trust, leverages diversity, fosters collaboration and teamwork, attracts and develops talent.

Leading with Vision

Key competencies: Focuses on customers, uses assertive communication, establishes relationships and networks, and influences and negotiates.

Leading for Results

Key competencies: Leads with vision, makes decisions, drives execution, and acts strategically.

Capability: Leading Self that comes from Sabio/Wise
Core Values of el Sabio: Trust, Pride, Faith

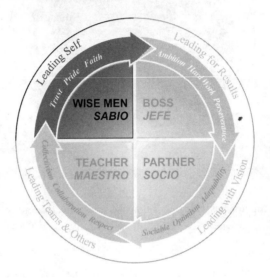

El Sabio is the Wise Person archetype in Latino culture; it is the role of *abuelitas* or *abuelitos* (grandmothers and grandfathers), older uncles, siblings, or close friends to whom the younger generation can turn for personal and professional advice. In a professional organization, these are the mentors who have the knowledge, experience, and connections. They are the older and wiser leaders who are in positions of power and who live ethical lives, both personally and professionally.

The el Sabio style of leadership is based on seasoned judgment, self-awareness, cross cultural competencies, and ethical management of people throughout the different constituencies in the company. Behavior grounded in trust, pride, and a spiritual belief system can foster those competencies. This style shows a tendency to display a more introverted attitude, rational thinking, and reliance on his or her own senses, as well as facts and figures when processing information and making decisions.

Trust

Trust is the cornerstone of Latino relationships, and comes from spending time with another person. Trust is the assurance that you know you can depend on another and rely on his behavior. It is built on sustained relationships and grows into loyalty and a committed employee. In Latin America, trust is reinforced if you know the other person's family and they have a good reputation. Latinos use the term *buena gente* ("good person") to describe a person who will do what he says he will do. Once broken, it is very difficult to reestablish trust with Latinos, so trust is a must when creating a relationship with this leader.

Pride

A Latino's pride is irrespective of his social position or the humbleness of his birth. With the increase in Latino population and the Latinization of the U.S., Latinos openly celebrate and take pride in their heritage. In many Latino barrios, individuals display their own country's flag. In the workplace, you often see flags on people's desks.

An affront against a person's pride can cause a deep emotional scar, and it can be difficult to recover from. It may be no more than a discriminatory look or gesture; it may also be an omission or lack of acknowledgement of his or her presence. A perceived insult affects Latinos on a deep level. This is important for el Sabio as he interacts with a diverse workforce. Acknowledging and respecting others' pride is the road to inclusion.

Faith

According to a survey from the Hispanic Churches in American Public Life, 70 percent of Latinos are Catholic and 23 percent are Protestant with about 85 percent of Latino Protestants identifying as Pentecostal or Evangelical. A belief in fate underlies most Latino religions or spirituality: Whatever happens is in God's hands, and Latinos know they will be cared for and protected. *Si Diós quiere*, "If God wills it or wishes it," is a common phrase that is applied to everything from air travel to whether tonight's stew will be tasty!

The belief in fate affects long-range planning as it relates to company benefits and 401k plans. More traditional Latinos totally believe the future is in God's hands, so why should they plan? This indicates a need for an educational component that clearly discusses company savings and health plans. The belief in God and the power of a larger force may be transferred to the boss, whom Latino employees trust to take care of them and their families.

Research suggests that a high level of awareness of one's strengths and weaknesses enables individuals to develop effective strategies for interaction and can help them to better respond to the demands of their environment. Successful Latino leaders' seasoned judgment is grounded in biculturalism, bilingualism, a diligent work ethic, and moral values. This judgment will inevitably be specific to their own culture, values, and principles and based on their own interests and experiences.

Latino leaders are culturally capable; they have a repertoire of culturally appropriate behavior, and they know when to use each approach. However, their thoughts, ideas, and points of view may be colored by their own cultural biases. It all begins when "leaders accept themselves and others" as they are, and as they are not. It is about learning from others who are not the same as us; it is about dignity and respect for all, and about creating workplace environments and practices that encourage learning from others and capturing the advantages of "all-inclusive" diverse perspectives.

Finally, mastering corporate politics without compromising one's values and ethics is an important competency. This is an especially important competency for Latinos and minorities in general to succeed in the workplace. Navigating the intrinsic corporate political culture is a complex competency to master and less relevant for organizations to measure, but it could make or break someone's career.

Capability: Leading for Results that comes from el Jefe/Boss
Core Values of el Jefe: Ambition, Hard Work, Perseverance

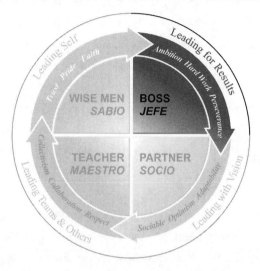

El Jefe is the Boss archetype in Latino culture. This role is primarily modeled by the mother, father, or other head of the family. El Jefe is an instinctive leader with a strong personality who is in charge and makes decisions. In a business setting, Latinos who are highly influenced by this archetype are individuals who are risk takers, driven, and ambitious. This person has individual aspirations and dreams along with the strong drive or passion to achieve. There are a number of strong Latina women in upper management positions, so el Jefe or la Jefa can be either male or female. This style shows a tendency to display a more extroverted attitude, rational thinking, but also to be and intuitive in his or her approach to processing information and making decisions.

Ambition

The 2010 *HACE Latino Professional Pulse*, conducted by the Hispanic Alliance for Career Enhancement, reported that Latino professionals seek growth opportunities and development.

32 percent have a graduate degree

19 percent are enrolled in an accredited graduate program

23 percent serve on a non-profit board of directors

Hard Work

Hard work can be a double-edged sword and may inhibit some Latinos from moving ahead. Hard work brings with it respect. When a person works beyond what is expected and is recognized for his diligence and tenacity, hard work is a good thing. But the ability to work smart sometimes eludes Latinos. If hard work takes the place of smart work, then Latinos can box themselves into a corner and they won't advance. Latinos acquire a strong work ethic from the el Jefe archetype. This model of hard work comes from seeing parents juggle two or more jobs to provide an education and opportunities for their children.

Perseverance

Many Cubans who try to escape to the U.S. in small boats are put in jail, only to try again and again. Many Mexicans courageously hike through tortuous heat and uninhabitable conditions to be turned away and try again another day. Each setback fuels the will of Latinos in the U.S. today to achieve their goals, knowing that they will have to work harder to persevere.

Capability: Leading With Vision that comes from el Socio/Partner
Core Values of el Socio: Sociability, Optimism, Adaptability.

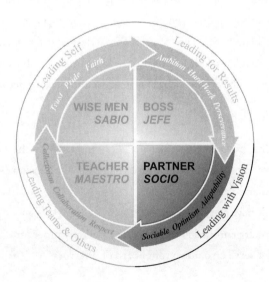

El Socio is the Partner archetype in Latino culture. The influence of this archetype comes from early exposure to frequent congregations where family topics are discussed or decided, always with the benefit of the group or family in mind. El Socio is about fostering relationships, support, and taking care of each other's needs. This archetype is expressed via social connections to other groups, for example, the church or other community organizations. In a business setting, individuals who are highly influenced by the el Socio archetype participate in Latino affinity groups and also want to foster participation with other, non-Latino groups to socialize and learn. These individuals are great at negotiations. They are optimistic, creative, service oriented, and adaptable stewards in their organizations. This style shows a tendency to display a more extroverted attitude, rational feelings, as well as being intuitive in the approach to processing information and making decisions.

Sociability

Latinos tend to have close-knit families that congregate frequently, which fosters el Socio's communal viewpoint. Most Latinos are friendly and nurture warmth in relationships. A social personality aids negotiations, builds strong customer service, and encourages a willingness to hear other's ideas, which leads to innovative thinking.

Optimism

In spite of the downturn in the American economy, Latinos tend to have an optimistic attitude about their future. This is especially true of immigrants. The *HACE Latino Professional Pulse* study reported that 72 percent of Latinos are positive about the future. Another factor that influences this attitude is the belief in fate and that one is in God's care. El Socio's optimism encourages and influences his or her colleagues by promoting positive energy.

Adaptability

When you come into contact with a new culture, you meet a multitude of new experiences that are as unpredictable as the weather. Language, food, transportation, communication styles, and corporate culture are just a few of these. This is especially true for ex-pats who come to corporate America as an adult to fill a management position. Not only do they need to be adaptable, but they also have to encourage their family to do the same. El Socio makes the new culture work for him because he is well versed in this adaptability. Does he miss the old ways? Yes, but because of a willingness and ambition to succeed, he will adapt and persevere.

Latinos are instinctively adaptable, sociable, and optimistic individuals with a strong focus on customer service. Working with different constituencies' points of view, needs, and opportunities will help them show their visionary capability to others, align people behind their vision, and rally people to support them. In general, Latinos have a cultural context wherein their communication style is indirect. They tend to give more details like personal stories and to be humble to the point of undermining their own contributions, in comparison with the corporate manner of being "brief, bold, brave, and to the point," which is perceived as more assertive.

To lead with vision, Latinos also need to develop assertiveness. The misconceptions that accompany a heavy accent contribute to this dilemma. Many of our clients come to us because they need to work on communication or assertiveness or performance reviews have continuously pointed the need to be more strategic. Managers in general need to become more culturally aware of these differences when evaluating performance, particularly styles of communication, leadership, and decision-making when working with multicultural and multilingual team members.

The willingness to help others will surface at times compromising the teams' purpose, outcome, or vision. In Latin countries, influencing and negotiation is expected of the person in charge, but the application of these skills in a corporate setting will take longer as trust and relationships build. Once trust and connection is established, Latinos are able to negotiate whatever issues come up in a highly effective way, but it is critical to understand that relationship precedes negotiation. This style of leadership is very appealing in a globalized, highly contextual business model in which more emphasis is placed on building longer-term business partners and forming social networks.

Capability:
Leading Others and Teams that comes from el Maestro/Teacher
Core Values of el Maestro:
Collectivismo, Collaboration, and Respect

El Maestro is the Teacher archetype in Latino culture. This role is played early by one's school teachers. El Maestro is caring, supportive, and imparts knowledge. The el Maestro archetype is in control of the group, but gives individual attention to learning, communicating, comprehension, and critical thinking. Quick to smile and warm-natured, el Maestro fosters collaboration and is a master at leading people. In a business setting, el Maestro is a subject matter expert, a leader who helps others to master a skill, and supports people who are trustworthy because they have proven their knowledge and proficiency. This style shows a tendency to display a more introverted attitude and caring nature, rational feeling, and sensitive approach to making decisions. When processing information, they need to see, feel, and touch facts and figures.

Collectivismo

Many of el Maestro's competencies come from his experience with family. Latino cultural framework expands the definition of family to include a much larger group than the nuclear family model that is familiar to mainstream

American culture. El Maestro has learned to develop a feeling of congeniality and friendship with others through the value of *collectivismo*, the importance of the extended family and greater community. He provides growth opportunities and is inclusive. This outwardly directed behavior attracts others to him, which builds confidence that this leader will do his best to see others succeed.

Collaboration

"Collaborate" includes the word "labor" and literally means "working together." A sense of collaboration is inherent in the Latino interpersonal dynamic. Because Latino cultural constructs support and value *collectivismo*, Latinos often prefer to work in groups. A desire to be with others fosters an ethic of cooperation and teamwork. Once again, this value originates from the extended family relationships that often go beyond blood relatives to other members of the Latino community. It is common to see large contingents from one geographic area in Mexico settle in a region of the U.S. because of a desire to collaborate with one another. El Maestro uses his collaborative nature to nurture inclusion and teamwork, and this strengthens the organization.

Respect

El Maestro values respect as an integral component of leadership, displays a high regard for all, and treats everyone as having personal honor and worth. El Maestro treats everyone with the same level of courtesy and consideration and does not differentiate based on class, job level, or service. Respect is a cornerstone for attracting and developing talent because it demonstrates the possibility that each employee has within the organization. For Latinos, respect is an affirmation of both a man and woman's honor, and as such, it is one of his or her most prized possessions.

In the context of leading teams, inspiring trust means having confidence about each member's ability, skills, and attitudes to better allow Latino leaders to assign suitable jobs, projects, or situations to match their skill set. Achieving this level of trust is difficult in a business context because people are taught to compete instead of to collaborate. Fostering teamwork, leveraging individual capabilities, respect, and collaboration are native competencies for the Latino leader and this creates a professional environment where people want to work with Latinos or have them as part of their teams.

The Leadership Pipeline

In their book *The Leadership Pipeline: How to Build the Leadership Powered Company*, Ram Charan, Stephen Drotter, and James Noel describe the six passages that mark every leader's career. It is critical for Latinos to understand these stages early in their careers as they relate to the Latino Competency Model in order to evolve their competency levels to align with the challenges of each career passage.

Managing other workers

After being in charge of only your own work, the first step toward becoming a manager includes planning, matching people to jobs, giving assignments, cheerleading, encouraging, helping, and evaluating. New managers often want to continue doing their old jobs; therefore, they may have obtained the title of manager but may not yet exemplify management behavior.

Managing other managers

This transition requires developing new ways of communicating and the understanding that now they must go through other managers to get things done.

Managing a function

When a person moves into functional management, he or she will manage some work that is unfamiliar and will report to multifunctional managers.

Managing a business

Most notably, the business manager must balance and harmonize numerous functions and work with a more varied set of people. This manager faces pressure to meet short-term financial goals while simultaneously thinking in terms of three-to-five-year plans. One common mistake during this passage is failing to respect staff functions.

Managing a group of businesses

The group manager must help make other people's businesses succeed and see that they get credit. It requires developing skills at allocating capital, developing other managers, thinking of the group as a portfolio, and making hard decisions about goals and capabilities.

Managing an enterprise

This transition requires being attuned to the values of the constituencies outside the corporation, such as regulators, the press, activist groups, and the public. The leader must assemble and coordinate a team of excellent subordinates.

Summary

Organizations need to identify strategies that are consistent with their organizational values, strategies, and goals to recognize that Latinos will perform differently depending on their individual value orientations, capability levels, and how well they accept, adapt, and integrate as they move up the corporate ladder.

Successful organizations establish a clear case for Latino leadership talent and assure that Latinos are well represented at each level including upper management. They promote Latino role models to demonstrate that success and upward mobility are possible and encouraged, and provide a range of developmental opportunities such as mentoring and coaching, developmental assignments, workshops, and conferences to develop the competencies described in our Latino Leadership Competency Model.

They develop a clear career path of progression within the organization that is visible and inclusive of all genders, races, and cultural groups. When it comes time for mentoring and coaching Latinos, they are mentored by other Latinos as well as non-Latinos. In addition successful organizations include multicultural development and cultural competencies as part of their professional development programs.

There is much more work to be done to explain what makes Latinos succeed and how they overcome challenges, negative stereotypes, and organizational cultural barriers. Mary Rowe, PhD from MIT in 1973 coined the word "micro inequity," referring to the ways in which individuals are singled out, overlooked, ignored, or otherwise discounted based on a characteristic such as race or gender. It generally takes the form of a gesture, different kind of language, treatment, or even tone of voice. It is suggested that the perceptions that cause the manifestation of micro inequities are deeply rooted and unconscious. The cumulative effect can impair a person's performance in the workplace, damage self-esteem, and may eventually lead to that person's withdrawal from the situation.

It is critical that executives strategically intervene to create more inclusive environments that encourage Latinos to advance in the organization. Highlighting best practices and sharing successful initiatives across companies and industries will create more cohesive and inclusive settings in which all groups can thrive.

CHAPTER 7

The Power of Networking and Mentoring

LATINOS approach networking differently from Anglos. Even though Latinos tend to be sociable, friendly, and gracious, they don't use these skills to network strategically. They acknowledge that networking can be advantageous, but at the same time, they tend to be skeptical of networking and see the process as a potential inconvenience to others or a waste of time.

Depending on their acculturation level and generation, Latinos are generally taught a strong work ethic from their parents. Implicit in this work ethic is that success comes from labor, not from relying on connections. They may view networking as political, shallow, egotistical, and superficial. Asking for help at work is perceived as weak, irresponsible, and a lack of respect for other people's time and attention. If this reluctance to ask for assistance is not detected early on by peers and bosses, Latinos will fail, without realizing their own role in the outcome. It is accurate to say that certain social constructs and values (i.e., humility, being part of a team as opposed to standing out) can make networking challenging for Latinos.

While Latinos are collaborators by nature, they can find it difficult to trust people outside their families. Less-acculturated Latinos may even experience animosity and distrust in an unfamiliar setting. Family members who may or may not have corporate experience often offer advice to leave the rat race and start their own companies, as Latinos are very entrepreneurial. Although this advice is well intentioned, it protects Latinos from confronting conflicts, overcoming the fear of rejection, managing humility and shyness, and nurturing confidence. This self-imposed isolation can often be a silent career killer.

Most of the top Fortune 500 companies have diversity and inclusion strategies to support diversity initiatives. In 2008 the Hispanic Association on Corporate Responsibility reported the failure of most common diversity programs that companies implemented to support Latinos.

Although diversity programs can increase job satisfaction and perhaps employee retention, respondents believe that salary, compensation, and benefits are the most important factors in hiring and retaining Latino talent. In our survey, *Latina as Corporate Leader*, conducted in April 2010, we asked respondents if their organization currently had a Latino resource or affinity group in place. Forty-two percent reported that they do, and 58 percent reported that they did not.

Of the organizations that employ a diversity program, many indicated some room for improvement. About 40 percent characterized it as extremely or very effective, and a further 40 percent rated it as only somewhat effective. When asked what changes, if any, could be made to existing Latino employee resource groups to improve working conditions, respondents offered the following needs in their written comments:

+ Further inclusion of Latino resource employees in decision-making, planning, and development of employee conditions.

+ Expansion of personal and professional learning from other groups. In general, the efforts tend to become silos at times, with departments cut off from each other.

+ Better leadership and accountability. The Latino community is frustrated because of lack of advancement. However, they are not willing to get involved and understand what they need to do or move forward to do it. They are waiting for someone to do it for them.

+ More education for the general public about the Latino community and their issues.

+ Increased executive sponsorship from senior management and more involvement from Latinos at higher levels who understand the strengths and vulnerabilities of Latinos in corporate America.

+ Additional orientation regarding corporate culture and how to handle difficult office politics without compromising integrity.

Employee resource groups

The value in formal network groups, affinity groups, or employee resource groups (ERGs) and Latino employee resource groups (LERG) is the ability to recruit, develop, retain, and advance an organization's talent pipeline; build commitment to diversity at all levels of the organization; promote its brand through its people; create awareness and education about Latino cultural traits, heritage and history; and actively connect with the community in which they do business.

ERGs can provide access to a network of peers who can offer valuable performance feedback in a nonjudgmental, non-threatening setting. ERGs can help future leaders learn new skills or hone the ones they have, as well as introduce them to the most senior executives in the organization.

Our experience and research tells us that a Latino resource and affinity group goes through at least four phases. During the evolution of the group it may integrate or combine some elements of these roles and strategic activities as it focuses on creating cultural advocates and talent development associates, becoming a trusted advisor, and reaching a desired level of business partners.

Figure 7.1   Latino Employees Resource Group Phases

Cultural Awareness Advocates	Talent Development	Trusted Advisors	Business Advocates
Social gatherings Celebrate heritage Sense of belonging	Mentoring and coaching Action learning Sharing with other resources groups Enhance professional development Assist with recruitment and retention	Benchmark outside the organization External alliances with professional organizations Talent pipeline advisors Collaborate with other groups Promote multicultural understanding	Enhance organizational capabilities by promoting new products or services Enhance brand image Develop community outreach programs Develop Latino market intelligence Positively impact the bottom line

Source: Life Coaching Group, LLC, 2010

Cultural Awareness Phase

Initially, the first phase's primary focus is to create social interactions through which employees can celebrate their heritage and create a sense of belonging to the Latino community within the organization. It occurs when a group of employees form affinity groups or associations or when, as part of their diversity and inclusion strategies, the organization decides to support an employee resource group. At this phase, it usually is not well structured and may have limited outreach and financial support from the organization. It is important to consider the support, resources, involvement of senior management, and the goals of the group.

Talent Development Phase

The second phase is one of talent development. It occurs when the group has been functioning for a while but is discouraged by lack of Latino involvement. The group then shifts toward becoming more talent-development driven. At this stage, the group engages the organization in events to mentor, coach, and develop its members.

The members' experience is used and leveraged as a call to action to get actively involved and promote the activities the group sponsors. The core team leading the group may open up to cross-pollinate learning from other diversity and inclusion groups or business units. Increased participation and commitment is instilled in its members to focus on enhancing professional development activities. For example, some groups invite guest speakers and experts on an array of topics. At this stage, the group may get involved in promoting recruitment activities. A team charter may be created to determine roles, responsibilities, and plans. It may include basic roles, responsibilities, and activities but may lack strategic alignment to critical business outcomes and clarity around competency-based, talent-development driven initiatives.

Our clients most frequently request mentoring and coaching programs that will support the development and advancement of a Latino pipeline. Here is an example of an approach taken by one of those clients.

LERGs Talent Development Phase Example

The Need

Accelerate the development of the Latino talent through the corporate pipeline into more senior management roles.

The Diagnosis

Challenges included a lack of mentors, and a lack of clarity about the roles and functions of those that acted as mentors. Mentors were all white men. It works best when there is a multicultural and cross-disciplined group of mentors from different background. The mentors had no sensitivity training on Latino values, putting Latinos at a disadvantage for upward mobility. Mentoring and coaching sessions were often called off at the last minute, and Latino mentees found it challenging to reschedule due to the mentors' busy calendars. There was no structure in place; if the mentoring session took place, it was informal, short, and rushed. Because no recognition or accountability measures were established, mentors did not see the value of their participation in the program. The Latino mentees felt discouraged and unappreciated, but fear prevented them from raising the issue with the human resources department.

The Solution

Life Coaching Group provided a fully integrated solution that combined the ERG's strategies with the Latino mentoring program. It involved the use of Insights Discovery tools and services, including the Discovery individual profile report on personality and preferences, facilitation, workshops, and one-on-one coaching to support personal and professional development of mentors, ERG members, and Latino employees. A communal approach to the mentoring program was established by including other groups that were focused on similar developmental needs.

The Results

The mentoring methodology is now the model for talent management in the organization and has become an integral part of many internal human resources processes. Diversity is included in the company motto, performance reviews, and reward system. Other resource groups and networks within the organization are being aligned to reflect a continuous mentoring model that furthers multicultural leadership development.

Trusted Advisor Phase

The third phase—becoming a trusted advisor—kicks in when the core team realizes it can play an advisory role and seeks to conduct surveys, research, and benchmark activities with professional organizations to share learning, best practices, and advice. Members of the group are called on to advise on talent management strategies geared toward the Latino workforce. Successful navigation of this phase requires a core group of mature leaders to promote high-potential Latino candidates for accelerated leadership programs and advancement regardless of personal interests. They must be focused instead on what is best for the organization and promotion of a multicultural talent pipeline. They should be looking for Latino talent that best exhibits the right ethics, capabilities, competencies, and skills.

One example is the outcome from our recent study, *Latinas as Corporate Leaders* in alliance with the National Hispana Leadership Institute (NHLI). Companies involved with NHLI took the survey to help develop a platform for specific leadership development workshops, career management seminars, and partnerships with women's employees resource groups.

Only 34 percent of the Latina NHLI respondents reported that there was a Latino Employee Resource Group (LERG) at their organization. Statistical comparison of individuals with and without a resource group provided evidence that the LERGs are providing benefits to Latina employees. For example, individuals with a LERG were significantly more likely to recommend others to work for their company, to report a higher level of overall satisfaction with their company, and to report higher levels of satisfaction with employee training and development.

Company size and LERGs

Latina respondents working for larger companies (those employing over 500 people) were more likely to report having a LERG than those working for smaller companies. In fact, almost half (47 percent) of those in large companies reporting having a LERG, compared with just 22 percent of those in medium-sized companies (50-500 employees), and 29 percent of those in small (fewer than 50 employees) companies. Interesting differences could be observed when looking at companies in one size category (small, medium, or large) and comparing those with LERGs to those without.

Large companies

In large companies with more than 500 employees, the Latinas with LERGs were significantly more likely to report being in a *higher income* category than those without LERGs. In large companies, the respondents with LERGs were significantly more likely to report being satisfied with their benefit packages than those without.

Small- and medium-sized companies

In companies with fewer than 500 employees, the Latinas with LERGs were significantly more likely to report that they would recommend that others work for the company.

Latinas with LERGs were significantly more likely to report being satisfied both with the training and development of employees, and also with overall satisfaction. This effect was very strong among Latinas working in smaller companies.

Latinas with LERGs reported significantly less *stress* than those without LERGs. This was in response to a question asking survey respondents to agree or disagree with the statement, "I feel under a great deal of stress on the job."

A specific data analysis technique allows researchers to examine a set of questions and pull out groups of questions that seem to be related, based on the way they were answered by the respondents. When this type of analysis was performed on the survey responses regarding attitudes toward the workplace, two separate groups of questions, called factors, emerged.

- Factor 1 included seven individual questions related to *tools, training, and information.*

- Factor 2 included six questions related to *respect, support,* and *empowerment.*

For example, there was a strong trend toward higher scores on Respect, Support, and Empowerment in large companies with LERGs, when compared to those without.

Each of these two factors seemed to tap something important about the respondents' workplace experiences. See a flash report below.

Figure 7.2   Latino employees resource group as a retention tool

Factor 1 Tools, Training, and Information	Factor 2 Respect, Support, and Empowerment
Latinas with LERGs scored their workplaces significantly higher on Factor 1, suggesting that they are more likely to feel they have the tools, training, and information they need to do their jobs.	Latinas with LERGs also scored their workplaces significantly higher on Factor 2, suggesting that they are more likely to feel heard, respected, and empowered than those individuals in smaller companies that do not have LERGs.

Source: Life Coaching Group, LLC, 2010

It's important to note that this type of research can't establish causation but it can help ERG groups to determine plans to advance to the second phase and strategically support talent development. In other words, we can't say definitively, based on this study, that the presence of a Latino Employee Resource Group *caused* the differences identified above. What we can say for sure is that the presence of an LERG *coincided* with these effects. It's possible that the LERGs are responsible for that difference, or it may be that some other aspect of the company (awareness of employee needs, or a desire to provide resources) leads to the creation of a LERG and also leads to the observed differences. However, it is clear that there are some important differences between companies with LERGs and companies without, and that these differences are particularly pronounced in companies with fewer than 500 employees.

In order to better understand the ways in which LERGs can be helpful to Latinas, we asked them, "What changes, if any, do you feel need to made in your Latino employee resource group to improve working conditions?" They had many ideas about possible changes.

Those who reported they lacked access to a LERG suggested starting one, or formally recognizing a group that had been meeting informally. Some acknowledged that they would likely face challenges in attempting to do so:

> "I only supervise one of the Latinos. The other director supervises the other five. I am not certain they would be interested or allowed to participate in a resource group."

Others identified a lack of resources as a problem:

> "The concept was initially well-received, then moved down the priority list as the budget crunch hit the agency. Volunteers have kept some things going, but this has become difficult to maintain."

A large number of Latinas who did not have an LERG in their workplace specifically mentioned a lack of diversity, particularly among leadership. This was frequently identified as a barrier.

> "I am the only bilingual assistant at our school's community college library. People of color need to be involved in my department's decision making."

> "Our organization is not very diverse; I am only one of two Hispanics at a Director level."

> "We really have a lack of diversity in the office that I work at. There is no person of color in the senior or mid-level management group. All the [people of color] are support staff."

Those who reported having an LERG also mentioned a lack of diversity at the leadership level specifically, and said they'd like to see greater involvement in the LERG from their managers.

> "More Latinos in upper leadership and administration. They are almost excluded."

"The resource group is a professional one of faculty and staff. It could use a greater level of support from the senior administration."

Some Latinas highlighted the need for increased participation and cooperation in an LERG from their fellow employees:

"The group needs to be expanded, it seems to be shrinking."

"More participation by Latinos. Quality participation by those involved."

"Less bickering and backstabbing amongst the participants."

Other Latinas felt their LERGs could benefit from increased communication and collaboration:

"We need to expand personal/professional learning with other groups . . . at times, the efforts tend to become silos."

"The resource group needs to network more on a statewide basis."

Finally, many of the Latinas addressed the issue of purpose for an LERG. Multiple individuals specifically mentioned a desire for fewer social and more professional activities. They identified many needs they felt an LERG could help them to meet:

"We don't need a group to put together a Chili Contest! We need a group that advocates for Hispanics to advance in the institution."

"Provide career development into higher graded positions. Latinas are significantly under-represented."

"Helping support stronger changes for work-life balance issues such as working from home options, flexible working arrangements . . . and partnering with HR to provide candidates for positions."

Business advocates

The last phase is the integration of key business drivers with the resource group's purpose to enhance the organization's capability to design, develop, and implement new products and services aimed at growth in the Latino marketplace. The focus is on key projects, business measurement, enhancing the brand, and becoming ambassadors of the employee value proposition in the community where they do business.

In 2007, Dow Jones News Service published an article titled "U.S. Food Companies Look for Growth in Hispanic Markets." The article highlighted several organizations, but the example provided by PepsiCo's spokesperson, Aurora Gonzalez, is most relevant to the discussion of how ERGs can reach business partners.

Frito-Lay, a division of PepsiCo, has fostered the development of its Adelante employee network, which is a multicultural Latino/Hispanic professional organization that helps develop a diverse, inclusive culture at PepsiCo. Gonzalez notes that Adelante, which is Spanish for "forward," "started as an opportunity for employees to connect, but has served in other capacities." Adelante is often a source of ideas for products, and Frito-Lay's marketing team sometimes runs new ideas by the group to find ways to make brands connect with the Hispanic community. "It's a back-and-forth kind of thing," said Gonzalez.

On March 11, 2009 Frito-Lay published an article on its blog titled "Reaching out to Hispanic Consumers" that detailed a new approach to developing Hispanic-inspired flavors. It now seeks guidance and input from the Adelante employee group to help lead innovation for the flavors of its new Hispanic-themed product line. "Adelante convinced Frito-Lay managers that they needed authentic flavors and snacks that appeal specifically to Hispanic consumers, the most rapidly growing population in the United States," says Marissa Solis, former president of Adelante.

Based on the authentic input from Adelante that Solis describes, Frito-Lay's marketing and research and development teams created six new snacks with flavor profiles that reflect Latino culture. These are primarily available in California, Arizona, New Mexico, Colorado, Texas, and Chicago—all geographic areas with a substantial Latino population. By involving the Adelante resource group, this organization engaged its Latino employees and its Hispanic consumers by including them in its research and development and marketing.

Frito-Lay's winning approach and Adelante's professionalism are great examples for other resource groups.

The future of ERGs

We are at a crossroads where the Latino older generations are required to stay longer at their jobs due to the economy and a younger generation, well educated and well acculturated, is entering the professional workforce, but somewhat naïve and inexperienced regarding the complexities of the workplace. The generation gap is widening as younger Latino professionals join the workforce. Here are some examples written by survey participants:

"There is a HUGE age gap. The younger Latino employees are not cut from the same cloth as those of us who are nearing retirement and have struggled within the business structure to create change. Most of them have no personal family struggle; they cannot relate to the issues we take to heart because no issues exist in their world."

"The problem the aging "catalysts" . . . NEVER do they take a stand to foster cooperative change for improvement . . . because they fear career suicide . . . Unfortunately, it is difficult to communicate with most of them (especially the females) because of the age gap and because they have assimilated into the urban educated young professionals."

"The younger staff with much more of their career ahead of them will not have learned what past struggles took place to create opportunity for them . . . there still are very subtle and systematic actions that occur. When it's brought to the attention of those affected, there is no desire to call attention to the action . . . they do not see it as an issue that needs to be brought up."

We see ERGs making a shift from cultural activities and outside guest speakers to occupying a more strategic role in their organizations' development and advancement of Latino talent. We witness these groups becoming more sophisticated participants of professional social networks like iHispano,

LinkedIn, Twitter, MySpace, Facebook, and WebEx. This change is due mainly to different networking opportunities that these new platforms provide in the form of posting issues and ideas or just having senior level management chats or productive group sessions.

We envision more robust financial support for these groups as their functions become more important to the businesses with which they are partnered, and as they become multicultural and cross-cultural forums for talent development where business strategies are discussed and leadership development and mentoring strategies take place rather than simply being a way to increase diversity and inclusion.

Summary

A robust employee resource group and a mentoring and coaching program for Latinos can facilitate their success within an organization and can also have a profound influence on their assimilation process, morale, engagement, and productivity. New technologies and shifting networking platforms may at first appear challenging, but they offer valuable opportunities for growth and communication. Organizations that employ these strategies will reap the benefits of increased employee satisfaction, the development of existing talent, and an appreciable contribution to their bottom line.

CHAPTER 8

MyBrand and Having a Voice at the Table

TWENTY-FIRST century corporations are restructuring, issuing pink slips, and asking each employee to contribute more. The trend is to make the corporate machine lean and efficient. Organizations are concurrently navigating generational and cultural differences. Never has it been more important for companies to develop Latino talent. Indeed, never has it been more important for Latinos to distinguish themselves in the workplace.

Companies can help Latino employees—and all their employees—to develop their personal brands through the *MyBrand* tools that follow. These will serve the company by helping it to use its talent most effectively and thereby increase revenue and profitability.

Making a place at the table

As corporate America hires Latinos, it should measure them against the same criteria as other new hires. Overall, once a Latino employee enters a company, his or her professional development should be the same as any other new hires. Yet managers need to recognize some of the cultural programming that Latinos bring to the table in order to help them grow and integrate into the company's unique business culture and workforce. This chapter gives managers a glimpse into Latino employees' cultural imprinting and how to help them maximize their potential by defining their unique MyBrand and cultivating their voices. MyBrand will show aspiring an Latino leader how to differentiate himself in the company so he will be seen and remembered.

Cecilia, a recent college graduate, was hired by an international cosmetics firm in New York that wanted to understand Latinas and develop products suited to Latinas. She was intelligent and personable, but it was the first time she had been away from her family and this was a difficult transition. Her parents had arrived from Mexico in the 1960s and raised Cecilia in Houston, a city that was experiencing growing Latinization. Though she had many non-Hispanic friends and felt integrated into the American way of life, Cecilia's Latino cultural imprinting affected her career growth.

Moving over a thousand miles away to New York City was the first time Cecilia had left her family for an extended period of time. Latinos want their families to stay together and don't like to see their children move away, even if they are adults. The separation from the family caused Cecilia to feel stressed and lonely.

Cecilia was taught to be agreeable, pleasant, non-confrontational, and humble. When she was asked for her opinion, she deferred to the group and didn't introduce an original idea. She was a follower, a role she had learned from observing her mother and aunts, which is characteristic of a Latina's *marianismo* role discussed in Chapter 3. Moreover, being humble is highly valued by Latinos and was a big part of Cecilia's upbringing. She was taught not to boast or brag about her accomplishments, but rather she should wait for others to mention her successes.

Cecilia's Latino heritage was important to this company because as a Latina, she represented the key target for its cosmetic line, and Latinas are big consumers of cosmetics. A study conducted by Simmons Research on behalf of Univision reported 69 percent of Latinas (versus 46 percent of non-Latinas) believe that "it is very important to wear makeup and look good." Moreover, 67 percent of Latinas (versus 50 percent of non-Latinas) cited their mother as the person who influenced them to take care of their skin, hair, or physical appearance. Seventy-three percent of Latinas agreed with the statement "I influence my children to take care of their skin, hair, and appearance." By comparison, 57 percent of non-Latinas agreed with this statement.

According to the book *Leadership Code: Five Rules to Lead By*, if a company wants to build effective leaders, it has to engage the talent and model leadership behavior. How did the cosmetics company do that, and how did it deal with these issues?

Placing numerous Latinas in high-ranking positions such as a member of the board of directors and chief marketing officer was a vital first step. The company also established HOLA, a Latino employee resource group that provided additional professional development to address the kinds of issues Cecilia faced. For example, the company had already instituted a flex-work plan, which allowed Cecilia to travel to Houston every two months, so she was able to work for the company as well as see her family. In addition, the company helped her understand that humility didn't serve her to develop a voice at the table. Through training and workshops, she was given the opportunity to assess her strengths, participate in role-playing to articulate those strengths in front of others, and create her personal brand.

These programs built Cecilia's self-confidence, and she was given a creative exercise to imagine a new product that would appeal to Latinas. Cecilia envisioned a line of tinted moisturizer foundations in multiple shades (for the many Latina skin tones), with increased sun protection for the sun drenched cities where many Latinas reside. She gained recognition from HOLA, caught the eye of the CMO, and sparked a new product for the company. She was on her way to becoming a leader.

Having a voice at the table

Latino business leaders will only advance if they develop a unique sense of self. Competition today is tough; many people have MBAs, foreign language proficiency, public-speaking expertise, computer skills, and strategic planning know-how. In fact, so many people have these talents that it takes a special effort to stand out. It is up to the Latino leader to develop an identity that differentiates him from the masses—the very definition of a personal brand.

Have you ever received a request from LinkedIn from someone you didn't recognize? Perhaps you vaguely remembered the name, but you couldn't place the person, even though the profile includes a photograph. This person has not succeeded in creating a personal brand.

How can Latinos use the power of their heritage to differentiate themselves from the masses? A personal story is a start. What was life like for your ancestors? What were the values, the *refranes or dichos* (familiar sayings) that you heard growing up? What are the life experiences? These elements form the foundation of a unique brand. Every person has an internal advantage that can never be copied by others.

As the choreographer Martha Graham said, "There is vitality, a life-force, an energy, that is translated through you into action, and because there is only one of you in all of time, this expression is unique. And if you block it, it will never exist through any other medium and be lost." For years, our parents have told us we are special. But why are we special? Certainly our fingerprints are unique, but that is merely a physical manifestation of our inner qualities. What truly creates our individuality is the sum total of our experiences, and this includes your heritage.

Personal experiences are the bedrock of a personal brand. Companies can use the MyBrand checklist to help employees define their brand:

MyBrand eight-point check list

1. What are the family stories that inspire you? Who have been your role models and whom do you want to please?

2. What are your interests and passions? What activities did you enjoy as a child and continue to enjoy today?

3. What are your strongest and weakest personality traits?

4. Where do you like to focus your growth and learning?

5. What skills do you want to develop?

6. What is your personal style? Sophisticated? Casual? Preppy? Trendy?

7. What is your energy level? Are you a fast mover or are you deliberate? Are you a morning person or do you work best late at night?

8. How do you communicate your desires and interests to others?

Creating a personal brand–MyBrand

A product will only succeed in the marketplace if it develops a brand that is memorable and reflects the essence of the product. Think about some of the brands you've grown up with—Coca-Cola, Pepsi, Cheerios, IBM, Apple, and Nike, for example. They've all created an expectation and an experience; you've formed a relationship with them, good or bad, and there is no doubt in your mind what you will get. In other words, they stand out.

People are also brands. When we hear the names Oprah, Sonia Sotomayor, Barack Obama, Abraham Lincoln, Osama bin Laden, or Shakira, we can visualize that person immediately; we have a clear understanding of what the person stands for, of his or her ideals and values.

In advertising and marketing, developing a brand is a complex process. A branding team is created that includes brand managers (from the company) and a creative team (from the advertising agency). They prepare a creative brief that includes the product's background, goals, attributes, benefits, brand promise, personality, style, packaging, and mission statement. A similar template can be applied to personal branding, and it works as an important step in knowing yourself on a professional level.

The next section is directed to Latino employees and will help form a bridge between the company and employees to engage them in the workplace and develop confidence. This exercise takes introspection and thought, but the payoff is that it forms the cornerstone of your ability to distinguish yourself.

To the Latino employee

How can you fill in the gaps to strengthen your brand? It may be making a conscious decision to perfect public-speaking skills. How did Cristina Benitez, one of the co-authors do this? First, she observed television, lectures, and conferences. She learned that a person's knowledge, enthusiasm, and authenticity make a speaker memorable and inspire action from the listener. Then, she went to Toastmasters and the National Speakers Association to learn from the pros and decide what aspects of their presentation skills she wanted to incorporate into her style. Next, she practiced; she even put on her "speaker's outfit" and rehearsed in front of a mirror, so she would feel comfortable with the flow, intonation, and timing. Then she created practice presentations and did them for friends, family, and colleagues.

Figure 9.1   MyBrand worksheet example

Date	Location

My Background	Core Values
My Latino Story: My father, Rafael Celestino Benitez and his family moved to New York in 1922 in an effort to gain a better education. The Benitez family was a leading family in the town of Juncos, PR. As one of the early waves of Puerto Ricans he and his siblings had to carve out their place in the new country. They all went to the university; my father went to the U.S. Naval Academy and later he met my mother, Nancy Shannon Critchlow, of Welsh descent. I am the eldest of three children and although we were all given Spanish names they were anglicized so that we would fit in during the 1950s and '60s. My name, Maria Cristina Benitez, became Crissie.	Family Respect Compassion Faith Health Honesty

Personality Attributes: "I am"	"I Am Not"
Authentic, Intelligent, Adventurous, Creative, Spirited, Curious, Social, Have a sense of humor	Shy, Pragmatic, Slow, Clandestine, Secretive

Key Business Attributes	Packaging
Leader, good communicator and listener, public speaker, technically savvy, good interpersonal skills, strategic thinking	Personal appearance, good grooming, style, physically fit, somewhat dressier than the mainstream

Personal Mission	Presentation Style
To embrace, respect and empower the Latino community. Lazos Latinos' mission is to provide clients with in-depth understanding of the Latinization of the United States, its values to the corporate world and its ability to develop and empower Latino employees to increase the bottom line.	Clear and knowledgeable public speaker, enthusiastic and passionate. Use good visuals, stories, and anecdotes to support key points.

Unique Selling Proposition	Tagline
Expert in the Latinization of the U.S. and its impact in marketing and leadership development.	Embrace-Respect-Empower

Now, take the time to create your own MyBrand. You want your name to be identified with your core values, passions, skills, and mission. Personal branding and creating MyBrand helps you to find the "core you," so you can put that into your professional growth toolbox. Have a friend take your photo (use your cell phone if you don't have a camera) and attach this to your worksheet as a visual component.

As with any product or service, there will be "new and improved" additions to your brand. Put the MyBrand exercise into your professional file. Take it out periodically and review it. Is it time to update it with new skills and aspirations? As change happens within your life, you will continually look at ways to reinvent yourself to stay current with what is happening in the world. Doing this also provides you with a resurgence of learning and energy, and as you evolve, so will your brand. Revisit and update MyBrand every couple of years.

The benefits of creating MyBrand are many. It builds self-confidence and provides a solid framework for how you lead your life inside and outside of the professional world. MyBrand also works within the family; it serves as a moral compass for your actions and how you teach your children and interact with members of your family. Besides your personal development at work, defining your own brand will also help you focus your interactions with the many professional and nonprofit organizations in your community where Latinos are needed. As you seek to develop your community service, use MyBrand to target your choices so you contribute your key attributes, passions, skills, and values to causes for the highest good of all concerned.

Your voice at the table

As a Latino leader, you take the lead in creating your personal brand, and you are responsible for "advertising" it. Promoting yourself takes many forms, from volunteering for special projects to participating in ad hoc committees and interacting at networking activities. All of these are worthwhile and necessary, but nothing is as valuable as being asked to participate in a meeting where your boss and his boss, maybe the CEO, are at the table.

If you have been asked to participate it is because you can contribute something of value to the meeting. At the early stages of your career, you may provide background information or presentation materials. As your position matures, you may provide innovative ideas or strategic thinking. However, being asked to the table is not the same as having a voice at the table.

This is where MyBrand will help you. Review your key skills, attributes, and values, and see how they apply to the subject being discussed. As you prepare for the meeting, familiarize yourself with the participants and what you know about their MyBrand. What motivates and makes them feel good about the company, the product, service, or the client? What are the outcomes they want? Once you've done the homework, decide how you want to contribute your unique advantage at the meeting.

This includes having a voice and speaking up. If you want to be a leader, you must demonstrate that you have leadership skills. This includes making intelligent contributions in order for your boss and others above him or her to notice you. Remember the example of not remembering some of the people who invited you to join their LinkedIn network? You must intelligently "advertise" your brand in meetings so participants will take note and remember you as someone who stands out. This includes dressing professionally and interacting with the other participants as a Latino leader. Arrive at the meeting early and go out of your way to introduce yourself to everyone there. Be sure to communicate your title, responsibilities, and accomplishments and in turn find out about the other people in the meeting. These relationships are your connectors to opportunities inside and outside the company.

Having a voice at the table makes it possible for you to highlight the unique contributions and diversity of the Latino community. Your innate knowledge and cultural imprinting can offer insights to your company as it seeks to increase its market share with Latinos.

It will be up to you as the "Latino expert" to dispel stereotypes. You may also find yourself up against prejudice, micro inequities, and negative attitudes about the Latino community. There are times when you will be expected to know everything about all twenty-two Spanish-speaking countries. Unfortunately, too many people in the United States have limited knowledge about international geography and history. Plan ahead how you might answer questions when you don't know the specific information. If you don't anticipate these situations, it can be tempting to sit back and become defensive, hurt, and angry about people's prejudices. Don't let that get in your way; rather, choose to help people understand Latinos.

It takes work, practice, and planning to develop a voice at the table. Only you can do it. Use MyBrand as a solid base to give you confidence, structure, authenticity, and power. Take the time this week to write out your responses to the MyBrand checklist and worksheet. Talk it over with family and friends, practice it, and then act it.

Figure 9.2   MyBrand Worksheet

Your photo here

Date   Location

My Background	Core Values
Personality Attributes: "I am . . . "	**"I am not . . . "**
Key Business Attributes	**Packaging**
Personal Mission	**Presentation Style**
Unique Selling Proposition	**Tagline**

CHAPTER 9

Latinas as Professional Leaders

LATINAS in the United States today are quite different from their mothers and grandmothers, says Leylha Ahuile, senior multicultural analyst at Mintel International. "Regardless of language preference, they have a new sense of self and the world around them. Whether she was born in the U.S., speaks only English, and has an advanced degree, she is first and foremost a Latina. Women that are newcomers to the U.S. and are Spanish-language dominant have a work ethic, combined with an entrepreneurial mindset that has surely changed the image they've had of themselves in countries that often offer few possibilities for these women."

The number of Latinas in the labor force has increased significantly, reaching 5.7 percent, of which 3.6 percent are employed in areas of management or other professional occupations. This may lead you to believe that advancing Latinas is a given. However, the reality is that Latinas are underrepresented in high-level jobs in Fortune 500 companies. Such companies have overlooked the fact that Latinas represent a significant talent pool. The number of Latinas with bachelor's degrees, master's degrees, and doctoral degrees have not only increased, they have surpassed those of their male counterparts. Despite their educational levels, Latinas are not making it to the top fast enough.

In this chapter, we will hear from three high-powered Latina leaders who show us how to succeed in corporate America. Their stories are both inspirational and no-nonsense, built on the tenets that you have to be excellent at what you do and be willing to take risks if you want to move up.

What does it take to make it?

"I felt I needed to start in sales, and aimed for the best company—Xerox. My goal was to be their best in sales."

—Maria Wynne, CEO, Girl Scouts of the Greater Chicago
and Northwest Indiana

Trend spotting, an irrefutable business sense, taking risks, persistence, and service: These are qualities of successful leadership. To really make it in the business world, the Latina executive has to use the same skills as other leaders, regardless of gender or place of origin. Simply put, you have to be good at what you do and have a relentless passion to fuel your goals.

Maria Wynne, CEO of the largest Girl Scout council in the U.S., the Girl Scouts of Greater Chicago and Northwest Indiana, started her career at Xerox after getting her MBA. In the late 1980s she spotted the growth in technology and knew this trend would lead her to a bright future. After a start in sales, Maria moved into management positions. Technology was moving away from analog, and Maria asked for systems training which she viewed as vital to becoming a senior leader. She was granted that training, which led her to managing a systems sales team.

Her success at Xerox caught the eye of an executive search team that tapped her for a role at Ameritech, the local Bell operating company, where she was charged with developing a new business model to reengineer the small business sales channels. She accomplished that re-engineering of channels across the Midwest, but as Ameritech was moving to implement the first outbound serving channel the budget was cut and the sales channel was outsourced. However, Maria's vision and connections led her to Moore Business Forms, now a part of RR Donnelley, where she developed a web-based, digital color output marketing service for one-to-one marketing, which was very innovative for its time. Her career came full circle when Xerox, aware of the web-based work Maria was doing, offered her a new position. By then she had been a general manager at Ameritech and held a senior director level at Moore.

Now she was focused on her next step, attaining responsibility at a vice president level. She let Xerox know that if she made her goals, she wanted the

VP position within three years of returning to the corporation. Maria was not risk averse. She excelled at her next job and was handily promoted to general manager in Pennsylvania, where she successfully headed an organization of 300 people for Xerox.

From there, Maria became the vice president in charge of establishing and managing the Xerox Services business in the U.S. public sector as the corporation was merging its mainframe and outsourcing businesses. She moved to Washington, D.C. to carry out that job and having accomplished it successfully, was then transferred to Chicago as the Vice President and General Manager for the Public Sector operation in the Midwest. Then the phone started ringing again.

Microsoft calling

Maria went to Microsoft in 2004 as the Business Marketing Officer to establish the position of field marketing. She created her new position as senior director of the Office of Citizenship and Innovation for the U.S. Public Sector of Microsoft, an organization dedicated to working with mayors of major U.S. cities to bridge the digital divide. She started with the Elevate Miami program (*www. elevatemiami.com*) and worked with Mayor Manny Diaz. With his support, she and her team took the fight for digital equality national. Mayor Diaz and Maria took Elevate Miami to the U.S. Conference of Mayors and the project continued to grow. After Maria left Microsoft, the National Governor's Association adopted Elevate America. This initiative provided one million vouchers for Microsoft e-learning courses and select certification exams at no cost to recipients. Elevate America was implemented in states across the country and helped train millions of people.

Networking with a nonprofit

By 2008, there were signs of an economic downturn but another opportunity was on the horizon. It was at a lunch with Hedy Ratner, cofounder of the Woman's Business Development Center in Chicago, that Maria was introduced to the idea of working in the nonprofit sector as the chief operating officer of the Girl Scouts. This job resulted in the unprecedented merger of seven Chicago area and Northwest Indiana councils that represented nearly 95,000 girls in 245 communities, creating the organization's largest council in the United States.

Maria Wynne attributes part of her success to supportive parents. Her Mom is Colombian and her father is part Colombian and part Welsh. "I was raised to be whatever I wanted to be. I was never told I had to follow traditional female roles, and I had family female role models such as aunts who were a biochemist, an opera singer, and a poet. Mom sought out schools that were very good for me." Maria learned that girls could be leaders and do anything. Her confidence was built early on at schools that taught critical thinking.

Maria Wynne operates from a number of career building principles: learn, master, and excel in the basics; have the vision to see trends and follow them to create the jobs you want; take risks but don't be willing to step back unless you have the opportunity to move forward; and do it all with integrity, brains, and grace.

Lighting the fire

"I went after it with a vengeance, backed by facts."

—Dolores Kunda, president and CEO, Lapíz

When Dolores started her career at Leo Burnett in the mid 1980s after graduate school, she worked in the general market. Because of her Spanish proficiency, she was tapped for a three-year assignment in Mexico City working on Kellogg's cereal business. At that time, the precursor to Lapiz, the Leo Burnett Hispanic Unit, existed as a service department within Burnett. Upon Dolores's return from Mexico she recognized the Latino market potential, and in 1993 she began her mission to convince management that The Hispanic Unit (which had a handful of employees at the time) should become an independent unit. It took six years, but in 1999 Lapíz was born. This major move was the result of Dolores's legwork: She created profit and loss statements to demonstrate that The Hispanic Unit was viable as an independent profit center. "If there is no business case, no one will listen to you," Dolores asserts. Today Lapíz is one of the leading Latino agencies in the U.S.

Dolores Kunda states emphatically that she was very lucky. "My family really valued education; my parents insisted that we set our sights on the best school and move away from home to attend college," she says. "They wanted us to experience the academic as well as the social education attained by moving away from home." It was good advice. Dolores moved from being a big fish in a small pond in high school to swimming with the big fish at Smith College. From there, she went to Washington where she became a business and financial reporter for F-D-C Reports, Inc. In this role, she reported the regulatory, legislative, and business news that affected the drug, biotechnology, medical, and health care industries.

One of the few females on the team, she was frequently outside her comfort zone and had to succeed in a male-dominated world. This experience helped Dolores fashion the business case to Leo Burnett Executive Management, and with their help, made Lapiz a reality.

The Journey is about service

"My mother taught me, it's all about service."

—Nora Moreno Cargie, director, Global Corporate Citizenship,
Boeing Chicago

Nora Moreno Cargie calls herself "Mexi-rican." Her father is Mexican, her mother is Puerto Rican, and their tumultuous marriage gave the role of parenting to her mother. Today, Nora is the director of Boeing's Global Corporate Citizenship office for Chicago, an organization that positions Boeing as a corporate citizen that provides both intellectual capital and corporate giving. She says Boeing sees itself as a community member that asks what Boeing and its employees can give back to improve lives and communities.

As one of five children who learned how to share with siblings and in the neighborhood, Nora watched her Puerto Rican single mom give back to the community. Her mother had obtained only a high school education, but she stressed the importance of education and was a hardworking entrepreneur. She opened the only minority-owned currency exchange in Chicago and believed that you should make money honestly and then give back to the community. Her mom created a special advice service at the currency exchange called "La Ventana de Consejos," or "The Window of Advice," where she provided financial planning and guidance to her customers. This example set Nora on her own path to success.

Nora's professional journey is one of service. She has worked with National Public Radio and the Chicago public school system; as deputy director of communications for Barack Obama's senatorial campaign; and as deputy commissioner for Chicago's Department of Human Services and the mayor's Office of Workforce Development. She led external relations for the Chicago Park District and Illinois Action for Children; and finally, Boeing, where she directs the company's programs to give back to the Chicago area communities. During an interview with Nora one cool, cloudy April day in Chicago, she said she asks herself, "What within this job can be better? How can I inspire and be inspiring?" Nora's philosophy supports that of other company executives who see making this world a better place for everyone as part of Boeing's responsible business practices.

Taking risks

Nora knew she was taking risks as she moved from one organization to the next—and that she would stretch into new roles and grow as a leader by doing so. When asked to do something different, she had the "I can do it" philosophy and was curious about how to improve the organization and make a difference. By taking risks, she knew she had nothing to lose and everything to gain, and she leveraged that perspective in every career decision. She worked hard along the way and always made a name for herself as smart, able to think on her feet, and a strategic planner.

Does being Latina matter?

Being Latina is very important to Nora Moreno Cargie, but she asks herself,

"How Latina can I be?" She's six feet tall and, in her own words, she is opinionated. "Latinas know how to package their strength to make it work," Nora says. "It's up to us to interact with colleagues, get them to know us better." She believes that you have to frame interactions to make everyone comfortable, to create those places where everyone can feel *simpático* with each other. Not always easy or possible.

Latinas breaking barriers

Much research has been focused on how minorities, especially Latinas, bring many valuable assets to the business world. In the article "Sin Fronteras," authors Hewlett, Shiller, and Sumberg corroborate that Latinas have an impeccable work ethic, a talent for collaborating with coworkers, and the cultural fluency necessary to succeed in corporate America. If Latinas are so valuable, why are they not in demand in the business world? Why are they underused? When they do hold jobs in lower management positions, what keeps them from climbing up the corporate ladder? Research seems to point to discrimination, isolation, family focus, work-life balance, and the fact that Latinas feel overlooked in business environments that are dominated by men.

Many Latinas have memories of parents and grandparents who went above and beyond in the workplace. The values of working with integrity and passion are ingrained in Latinas, as are respect and loyalty. These characteristics make Latinas ideal members of any corporate team. They come from an array of cultures in the U.S. and Latin America, which makes them respectful of other cultures. Many Latinas are bilingual, and their cultural constructs provide them with a strong sense of family and community; these attributes allow them to act as valuable bridges between corporations and the communities they serve.

Dolores Kunda says, "The truth is, I don't feel that I was ever denied anything for being Latina or a woman. I never felt that I was overtly discriminated against." Dolores made up her mind that when she wanted something, she would go after it with a vengeance, backed by facts. She admits that it's very hard to navigate politics. "I don't like it but I have to do it, especially as the head of a company. I feel committed to my people and I take their interests to heart. To navigate politics, one has to realize that the process may not be the most efficient, and many times you can't say what's truly on your mind. But one of my favorite quotes is, 'From those to whom much is given, much is expected.'"

Are women leaving the corporate world? "Yes, some companies have a tough environment and may not offer a support system for women," says Maria Wynne. She goes on to comment, "More male-dominated fields—engineering, the sciences—may not have the support system. Then there is the issue of balance. Men usually only need to feel success in one area, whereas women feel they need balance in a variety of areas."

Latina entrepreneurs

Firms that are owned by a majority (51 percent or more) of women of color represent an estimated 1.9 million businesses in the United States. An estimated 642,458 (33.8 percent) majority-owned, privately held firms owned by Latinas in the U.S. generate $45 billion in sales. Nearly 40 percent of all Latino-owned firms are owned by women.

Latinas are the fastest-growing business segment in the United States. In response to this fact, the United States Hispanic Chamber of Commerce created a Latina Initiative to promote procurement opportunities for Latina-owned businesses and to develop leadership skills. At its 2009 annual convention in Las Vegas, it celebrated outstanding Latina businesses at the first USHCC Latina Summit. The theme, "Building the New Economy with the Help of Latina Entrepreneurs," focused on the achievements of women in industries that are not traditionally female oriented.

Latinas are also being recognized in government. Hilda L. Solis was nominated by President Barack Obama to serve as Secretary of Labor. President Obama also tapped Sara Manzano-Diaz to be the 16th director of the Women's Bureau at the U.S. Department of Labor. In this role Ms. Manzano-Diaz seeks to improve the status and working conditions of wage-earning women, increase their efficiency, and advance their opportunities for profitable employment. Latinas face several challenges in the workplace:

* stereotypes that might prevent them from getting a promotion,

* isolation,

* the belief that promotions are based on appearance not merit, and

* lack of trust.

An exemplary Latina entrepreneur:
Teresa Zubizarreta (1937–2007)

Teresa Zubizarreta was born in 1937 in Cuba, came to the U.S. in the 1960s, and created an advertising agency that prides itself on erasing stereotypes. A visionary in Latino advertising, Teresa Zubizarreta founded Zubi in 1976. Zubi became one of the largest independent, privately held, and minority-owned advertising agencies in the country with over 30 years of creating award-winning campaigns for nationally known companies, including American Airlines, Ford Motor Company, Olive Garden, Chase, S.C. Johnson, The J.M. Smucker Company, and Winn-Dixie. In 2009, Zubi had projected billings of $175 million. The agency Teresa created is now headed by her son, Joe, and employs 122 individuals who honor her legacy of enhancing the image of Latinos.

What can organizations do?

In 2005, the Network of Executive Women from the consumer packaged goods industry met to develop the "New Latina Agenda." This group of high-level executives from companies such as Procter & Gamble, Kellogg's, Sara Lee, PepsiCo, Hershey's, Wrigley, and others met in a two-day conference to discuss such topics as what Latinas bring to the workplace, earning power, work-life balance, stereotyping, recruitment, retention, and advancement of Latina leaders. They published a white paper titled *Latinas: Opening Doors to New Opportunities*. Some of these companies have created forums, specialized programs, workshops, and awards that show their commitment to Latinas. These are all excellent examples of proactive steps toward advancing Latinas.

All companies should be concerned with recruiting and retaining Latinas.

But it is essential that companies instill trust, provide ways for their Latina executives to exercise the good leadership skills they possess, and provide an environment that nurtures success. Businesses can provide opportunities to connect with other people in their field, socialize with coworkers, and create a sense of sisterhood among women who might otherwise feel isolated. Having role models, mentors, and business coaches are ways to develop Latina employees and create the leaders of the next generation.

Dolores Kunda believes it is the responsibility of senior leadership to provide guidance and mentoring programs for younger employees. They need help to develop thicker skins and realize that not all critiques are personal. The trick for senior executives is to find the time to thoughtfully mentor the new hires in between taxing workloads and putting out fires.

Girl Scout CEO Maria Wynne says, "The culture needs to reflect that within the company women and women of color are valued. Why aren't there more women on the boards of directors? Companies need to demonstrate they are mirroring the demographics; a boardroom shift needs to happen. If performance is there, managers should invest time and help develop talent."

Organizations need to progress from a conversation about the difficulties of retention to implementation and actualization of policies, procedures, and organizational structures that get the job done. It's about sharing best practices and learning from each other. Companies need to welcome, engage, and respect their diverse talent pool; recognize the abilities and values they bring to the organization; and provide opportunities for career development.

Highlights from Latinas as Corporate Leaders Study

The leadership stories of these outstanding Latina leaders support the work in our study, *Latinas as Corporate Leaders*. We surveyed 275 Latina professionals to build awareness among organizations about Latina professional attitudes toward work and career, their employment satisfaction, and their compensation and benefits. This was possible with the support of the partnership with the National Hispana Leadership Institute.

Value Latinas' unique skills

Several Latinas who responded to the survey noted that they often use their bilingual skills, responding to requests for translation or communication even outside of their own department. However, many noted that their companies seem unaware of the value of their language skills. And yet when a Spanish-speaking customer needs assistance, or a letter needs to be translated, or publicity needs to be designed for a Spanish-speaking audience, employees seek out their bilingual colleagues for assistance. Be sure that you are aware of your bilingual employees, and that their bilingual and bicultural skills are recognized as an asset.

Latinas' education and employment

The Latinas responding to this survey are much better educated than their parents were—about 70 percent of their parents received a high school diploma or (often) less. But among the Latinas responding to the survey more than 40 percent had graduate degrees. Clearly, Latinas are becoming increasingly educated, although this doesn't always appear to translate into executive-level jobs, as Latinas remain woefully under-represented at that level.

In regards to college education, there seems to be a split at approximately age 40 among the Latinas surveyed. Latinas who are younger than 40 are significantly more likely to have a college education. This isn't to say Latinas above age 40 do not have college degrees—among those who responded to this survey, 83 percent of Latinas over age 40 reported having a college degree. However, an amazing 97 percent of the Latinas age 40 and under reported having college degrees. Latinas clearly recognize education as important, and they are taking advantage of educational opportunities that are open to them.

However, they still appear to be struggling to translate their education into high-level employment. Approximately half the women with master's degrees reported that their job requires only a bachelor's or less. It may behoove employers to ensure that Latinas, who have shown a willingness to invest both time and money in their education, are provided with training and opportunities to advance themselves in the workplace.

Factors influencing workplace perceptions

Because groups of questions are widely recognized as providing more accurate information than individual questions, the two factors that emerged from this research constitute valuable information about Latinas' perceptions of their work environment.

+ Factor 1 taps Latinas' perception that they have the training, tools, and information they need to be successful in their jobs.

+ Factor 2 taps Latina's perceptions that they are heard, respected, and empowered in the workplace.

Both factors were related to the Latinas' sense of satisfaction with their jobs, as well as their willingness to recommend that others work for the company. However, it's important to note that Factor 2 seemed to have a particularly important relationship to job satisfaction. It appears that the Latinas who responded to this survey feel strongly that being heard, respected, and empowered in the workplace is vital to their job satisfaction. Comments by the Latinas support this conclusion, as the features tapped by Factor 2 were well-represented in both their suggestions for improvement and their favorite aspects of the job. Several of the women identified flexibility, autonomy, respect, and a sense of being valued in the workplace as being particularly important to their experience.

It's also possible that this kind of environment would naturally lead to better outcomes in Factor 1, which measured the Latinas' sense that they had the tools, training, and information necessary to do their jobs. If management creates a supportive environment that values each member of the workforce, it will also likely be more aware of its employees' need for the necessary training and information than companies who do not create as supportive an environment. In trying to foster an environment that supports and empowers all members of the workforce, companies can look to the following areas:

+ Ensure that employees have a voice in major decisions.

+ Treat all employees fairly and with respect.

+ Provide flexible work arrangements, and recognize the importance of a healthy life-work balance for employees.

+ Ensure that all employees' skills and abilities are recognized and used.

+ Continue to develop employees' abilities through training and development programs.

Company size and Latino employee resource groups (LERGs)

As we discussed earlier, Latinas benefit the most from LERGs. Companies of different sizes face very different challenges in developing a supportive workplace for Latinas. Larger companies are often able to pay higher salaries and provide better benefit packages, but it is more difficult for them to ensure that Latinas feel valued in the workplace, or that they are satisfied with their jobs.

This study showed that a Latina Employee Resource Group can help Latinas feel heard, valued, and empowered. Because some companies or departments may not have enough Latinas to support a LERG, it might be necessary to find alternative ways of organizing across companies, perhaps using online technology to make connections with Latinas in other departments, companies, or regions. Future research might compare companies where LERGs already exist with companies where they have not yet been formed. There may be other important features of these companies that lead to positive results for Latina employees, for instance:

+ coaching and mentoring programs,

+ career counseling sessions,

+ career management workshops,

+ flexible work hours or schedules,

+ specific leadership development programs,

+ increased visibility through key assignments, projects or teams,

+ use of latino community outreach programs as a developmental tool,

+ encouragement and support for active participation in not-for-profit boards,

+ tuition reimbursement or loan programs to foster higher levels of education, and

+ informal chats on how to succeed at work, politics, and corporate culture aligned with your industry or company.

In small or medium-size companies with fewer than 500 employees, the presence of a LERG can make a significant difference for employees in many areas. Latinas with LERGs reported greater job satisfaction, lower stress levels, and higher ratings on both Factor 1 (tools, training, and information) and Factor 2 (support, respect, and empowerment). The effect on Factor 2 was particularly strong, which suggests that it may be easier for a small company to make a significant change in its environment with the addition of an Employee Resource Group for Latinas. Again, it might be worthwhile for future research to explore the differences between companies with and without LERGs, as there could be institutional factors that are independently contributing to Latinas' satisfaction and empowerment (separately from the presence of a LERG).

Finally, a number of the Latinas specifically mentioned a lack of diversity in their companies, particularly at management or executive levels. They expressed a strong desire for more training and mentoring that would allow them to advance within the workplace. It was remarkable how often the words "team" and "family" came up in Latinas' descriptions of positive work environments. Their responses seem to indicate a strong desire for (and appreciation of) a supportive, collegial atmosphere in which they feel known and valued as both people and employees.

Latinas are demonstrably eager to be successful and advance in the workplace, and they look to initiatives like LERGs to take a more active role in their professional development by providing the training, networking, and support they sometimes feel is lacking. As Latinos and Latinas continue to grow and increase their presence as consumers, workers, and employers, those organizations that do not adapt to changing demographics will see their products and effectiveness suffer as a result. Those who successfully recognize and advance Latina employees and use their skills in reaching out to the broader population will maintain a strong foundation as they move into the future.

Summary

Employers have limited resources, and it's important to invest them wisely in ways that will be most beneficial to the company. And indeed, companies will see huge benefits from investing in efforts to both appeal to the quickly growing Latino market and also take advantage of the growing population of highly motivated, well-educated Latina workers. Organizations that manage this challenge successfully will find themselves in a position of strength both nationally and internationally, able to adapt easily to the demanding task of navigating the increasingly invisible—yet always important—boundaries between cultures and nations.

Latinas are one of the fastest-growing groups of women in the U.S. labor force, but remain among the least represented in top positions at Fortune 500 companies. While Latinas represent 3.6 percent of all people employed in management, professional, and related occupations, they hold only 0.3 percent of corporate officer positions in the Fortune 500 (Diversity at Work, 2010).

Latinas are working hard to close that gap, earning university and graduate degrees at an astonishing rate. The number of Latinas earning bachelor's degrees increased an amazing 222 percent between 1996 and 2006, which was larger than the rate of increase for any other racial or ethnic group. The number of Latinas earning master's degrees increased 307 percent over the same time period (Hewlett, Shiller, & Sumberg, 2007).

Still, the quickly changing labor market can leave executives struggling to understand how best to build a flexible foundation for success in the workplace, recruit and retain the best possible employees, and support promising individuals in developing leadership abilities. Although they are finding employment in growing numbers, Latinas face many challenges in the American workplace. Among them are a lack of access to mentors and networking opportunities, stereotypes and stigma, a lack of respect for their family obligations, and a need for more flexibility in the workplace. These challenges may lead Latina executives to become less invested in their work and potentially leave a job behind. The Center for Work-Life Policy found that almost 50 percent of young (under age 40) women were actively considering quitting their jobs, often as a result of the issues mentioned above (Hewlett, Shiller, & Sumberg, 2007).

Selected Resources

(Parentheses indicate chapters where these sources served as references.)

Books

Burt, R. S., *Social Origin of Good Ideas*, Chicago: University of Chicago and Raytheon Company, 2003. (Chapter 7)

Covey, Stephen R., *The 7 Habits of Highly Effective People*, New York: Free Press/Simon & Schuster, Inc., 2004. (Chapter 3)

Charan, Ram, *The Leadership Pipeline; How to Build the Leadership-Powered Company*, San Francisco: Jossey-Bass, 2000. (Chapter 6)

Goleman, Daniel, (1997). *Emotional Intelligence: Why It Can Matter More Than IQ*, New York: Bantam Dell Publishing Group, a division of Random House, Inc., 1997. (Chapter 3)

Harris, Philip R., *Managing Cultural Differences*, Burlington, MA: Elsevier Butterworth-Heinemann, 2004. (Chapter 7)

Huntington, S. P., *Who Are We? The Challenges to America's National Identity*, New York: Simon & Schuster, 2004. (Chapter 5)

Knouse, Stephen B., *Hispanics in the Workplace*, Newbury, California: Sage Publications, Inc., 1992. (Chapter 7)

Misner, Ivan R., *Masters of Networking*, Marietta, Georgia: Bard Press, 2000. (Chapter 7)

Sawyer, Keith, *Group Genius: The Creative Power of Collaboration*, New York: Basic Books, 2007. (Chapter 2)

Shirky, C., *Here Comes Everybody*, New York: Penguin Press, 2008. (Chapter 7)

Tapia, Andrés, *The Inclusion Paradox: The Obama Era and the Transformation of Global Diversity*, Hewitt Associates, 2009. (Chapters 2, 6, 7)

Ulrich, Dave, Norm Smallman, and Kate Sweetman, *The Leadership Code: Five Rules to Lead By*, Cambridge: Harvard Business School Press, January 2009. (Chapter 8)

Wyche, K. R., *Good Is Not Enough*. New York: Penguin Group, 2008. (Chapter 7)

Journals

Arroyo, Raymond J., "Achieving Professional Success Matters, But not As Much as Personal Success: A Conversation with Admiral Joxel García," *The Business Journal of Hispanic Research*, Vol. 2 No. 3, 10-17. 2008. (Chapter 2)

Gallegos, P.V. and B.M. Ferdman, "Identity Orientations of Latinos in the United States." *The Business Journal of Hispanic Research*, Vol. 1, No. 1, 2007. (Chapters 5, 6)

Gentry, William A., Phillip W. Braddy, John W. Fleenor, and Pierce J. Howard, "Self-Observer Rating Discrepancies on the Derailment Behaviors of Hispanic Managers," *The Business Journal of Hispanic Research*, Vol. 2 No. 1, 2008. (Chapter 6)

Gluszek, Agata and John F. Dovidio, "The Way They Speak: A Social Psychological Perspective on the Stigma of Nonnative Accents in Communication," *Personality and Social Psychology Review*, Sage, March 2010.
(Chapter 5)

Lev-Ari, Shiri and Boaz Keysar, "Why don't we believe non-native speakers? The influence of accent on credibility," *Journal of Experimental Social Psychology*, Chicago: The University of Chicago, 2010. (Chapter 5)

Thomas, David A. and Robin J. Ely, "Making Differences Matter: A New Paradigm for Managing Diversity," *Harvard Business Review*, September-October 2006. (Chapter 3)

Savage, David. "Race Runs Through Files," *Chicago Tribune*, June 5, 2009. (Chapters 5, 6)

Miscellaneous

Benitez, Rafael C., Associate Dean of the School of Law, *The Character & Values of the Hispanic American*, President's Program for Spanish-Surnamed Americans, University of Miami, September 1972. (Chapter 6)

Catalyst Quick Take on Latinas, New York: Catalyst, 2009. (Chapter 9)

HACE Latino Professional Pulse, "Making a Difference: Attitudes and Characteristics of Today's Latino Professionals," Hispanic Alliance for Career Enhancement, June 2006. (Chapter 6)

HACR Corporate Governance Study 2008. (Chapter 4)

National Community for Latino Leadership, "Reflecting an American Vista: The Character and Impact of Latino Leadership." (Chapter 3)

National Hispanic Christian Leadership Conference, "Latino Religion in the U.S.: Demographic Sifts and Trends—'Pentacostalization' takes hold among Latinos; Catholic Church Remains Strong, April 2006. (Chapter 6)

Selig Center for Economic Growth, Terry College of Business, The University of Georgia, July, 2007. (Chapter 1, 2)

The Network of Executive Women, *Latinas: Opening Doors to New Opportunities*, Chicago, 2008. (Chapters 5, 9)

Tomás Rivera Policy Institute, *Increasing Wealth in the Latino Community*, 2007. (Chapter 1)

Fiscal Policy Institute, *Immigrants and the Economy: Contribution of Immigrant Workers to the Country's 25 Largest Metropolitan Areas*, December 2009, http://www.fiscalpolicy.org/ImmigrantsIn25MetroAreas_20091130.pdf (Chapter 2)

Pew Hispanic Center, Washington, D.C.

Between Two Worlds: How Young Latinos Come of Age in America, December 11, 2009. (Chapter 6)

Country of Origin Profiles of U.S. Hispanics, October 15, 2009. (Chapter 2)

Latino People in Motion, 2005. (Chapters 3, 8)

Latinos in Higher Education; Many Enroll, Too Little Graduate, by Rick Fry, September 5, 2002. (Chapter 3)

Occupational Attainment and Mobility of Latinos in a Changing Economy, by Maude Toussaint-Comeau, Thomas Smith, and Ludovic Comeau Jr., 2005. (Chapter 3)

Statistical Portrait of Hispanics in the United States, 2008. (Chapter 3)

U.S. Population Projections: 2005–2050, February 11, 2008. (Chapter 2)

U.S. Government

Bureau of Labor Statistics, weekly earnings report of wages and salary, 1st quarter 2010. (Chapter 4)

Bureau of Labor Statistics, *A New Look at Long-term Labor Force Projections to 2050*, by Mitra Toosi, 2006. (Chapter 3)

Bureau of Labor Statistics, *Labor Force Projections to 2016: More Workers in Their Golden Years*, by Mitra Toosi, 2007. (Chapter 3)

U.S. Census Bureau, *U.S. Hispanic Population*, 2008. (Chapter 3)

U.S. Census Bureau, Interim population projections released 2008 and annual July 1 population estimates. (Chapter 1)

U.S. Census Bureau, *The American Community Survey 2008*, Table 7, Nativity and Citizenship Status by Sex, Hispanic Origin, and Race: 2008. (Chapter 2)

U.S. Department of Commerce, Economics and Statistics Administration, *Income, Poverty, and Health Insurance Coverage in the United States: 2008*, by Carmen DeNavas-Walt. (Chapter 5)

U.S. Office of Personnel Management, "Eighth Annual Report to the President on Hispanic Employment in the Federal Government," December 2008. (Chapter 4)

Index

About the Authors

MARLENE GONZÁLEZ, is founder and president of Life Coaching Group LLC. She is a leader in the cutting edge industry of executive coaching, consulting, and training. Her organization is dedicated to "developing leaders as a catalyst for corporate growth and a source of intellectual capital." Her client list includes government, non-profit, educational institutions, and Fortune 500 companies. She supports them in areas such as multicultural leadership, gender equality, and women's empowerment, mentoring, and coaching programs, career development, wellness revolution, managing cultural differences, and building cross-cultural teams. She serves on multiple boards and non-profit organizations, including as a board member for National Council of La Raza, National Hispana Leadership Institute, and the National-Louis University. Her company's website is: *www.lifecoachinggroup.org*.

González has more than 30 years of corporate and business experience with Fortune 500 companies. She held many executive corporate positions in the U.S., Europe, and Latin America in areas such as management, operations, product development and innovation; franchising and field service, training, learning and development. She is the former senior director of global training, learning and development for McDonald's Corporation. She led the strategic execution of the global training strategies, executive development and learning technology platform for the entire enterprise that supported 2.5 million employees in 30,000 restaurants located in more than 140 countries; in addition, she partnered with six corporate and local universities for curricula accreditation and alignment in 5 continents in more than 40 languages.

González is a certified Executive Coach, Life Wellness Instructor, and is a licensed practitioner for the Insights Discovery personality assessment model. She holds a BS degree, an Executive MBA/PAG from IESA Business School in Venezuela, and also holds a graduate diploma on managerial issues in the global enterprise from Thunderbird University, the Graduate School of International Management in Phoenix, Arizona. She is pursuing a doctorate degree on Natural Health and Nutrition.

González has been a recipient of many awards and recognitions such as Cambridge Who's Who among Executives and Professionals, the President's Award for a Fortune 500 company, Team Awards, Manager of the Year, and was named one of the Top 100 Executives in Latin America by *Dinero* Magazine. She resides in Illinois with Carlos, her husband of more than 20 years; they enjoy traveling, and gourmet cooking.

About the Authors

CRISTINA BENITEZ is an Hispanic market specialist. For nearly three decades, she has developed a wide range of branding and marketing programs that target the growing Latino population in the United States. In 2010 she was appointed Director of Latino Media and Communication, an undergraduate and graduate program, at DePaul University in Chicago. She is also an entrepreneur and in 1998 founded Lazos Latinos, a specialty Hispanic, strategic branding and advertising company based in Chicago.

Formerly senior vice president of ethnic marketing at DraftWorldwide, Ms. Benitez directed Hispanic direct marketing campaigns for Sprint, AARP, PacifiCare, HFC and Miracle-Ear. While at Draft, she spearheaded Dimensión Draft, the agency's nationally recognized study on Hispanics and direct marketing. This research was the first of its kind to examine direct opportunities targeting Hispanic consumers. Cristina's prior Hispanic advertising experience was VP Account Services at FOVA, Grey Advertising's Hispanic agency in New York. In this capacity, she introduced many products into the Hispanic market such as Cover Girl, Pantene, Kraft General Foods, and Dannon Yogurt among others.

In 2005 Ms. Benitez's company, Lazos Latinos, added "Latinization" to help Fortune 500 companies understand and develop their Hispanic employees. Her workshops, Linking Latino Values to Leadership, have helped companies such as Deloitte, Kraft, P&G, Abbott, Exelon, General Electric, PepsiCo, and Shell to name a few. Cristina's expertise across all aspects of advertising, her passion for Latino leadership development, and her culturally diverse background as a bilingual native of Florida make her an invaluable and highly successful motivational speaker.

In 2007 Paramount Market Publishing released her first book, *Latinization: How Latino Culture is Transforming the U.S.*, which was their best selling book of the year. Latinization and the Latino Leader furthers her goal of empowering Latinos in the United States.

Ms. Benitez lives in Chicago with her husband and is active civically as a Board Member of The Chicago Public Library, The Gateway Foundation, The Luna Negra Dance Theater, and serves on the Audience Development & Diversity Committee of the Museum of Contemporary Art. She created and taught Hispanic marketing at Columbia College Chicago; is a frequent speaker at national conferences on "Trends in the U.S. Hispanic Market," "The Latinization of the United States," and "Harnessing Latino Influence for Employee Development."

In November 2008, Ms. Benitez was a recipient of the 2008 ATHENA award for assisting women in achieving their full potential and providing opportunities for the growth and development of women owned businesses. In September 2009. Ms. Benitez received the Latino Author's award from Illinois Secretary of State, Jesse White, at the state's 2009 Hispanic Heritage event. She loves to play the piano, dance, travel, and visit family including her son and his wife in Colorado. Her website is *www. lazoslatinos.com.*